2002–2003 Annual
Supplement to

THE PIANO BOOK

BUYING & OWNING A NEW OR USED PIANO

LARRY FINE

BROOKSIDE PRESS • BOSTON, MASSACHUSETTS

Brookside Press
P.O. Box 178, Jamaica Plain, Massachusetts 02130
(617) 522-7182
(800) 888-4741 (orders: Independent Publishers Group)

info@pianobook.com
www.pianobook.com

Printed in the United States of America

Distributed to the book trade by Independent Publishers Group,
814 North Franklin St., Chicago, IL 60610
(800) 888-4741 or (312) 337-0747

ISBN 1-929145-08-X (print edition)
ISBN 1-929145-09-8 (electronic edition)

NOTICE

Reasonable efforts have been made to secure accurate information for this publication. Due in part to the fact that manufacturers and distributors will not always willingly make this information available, however, some indirect sources have been relied upon.

Neither the author nor publisher make any guarantees with respect to the accuracy of the information contained herein and will not be liable for damages—incidental, consequential, or otherwise—resulting from the use of the information.

INTRODUCTION

Given the long time span between new editions of *The Piano Book,* it's impractical to provide in the book itself the detailed model and price data that piano shoppers increasingly seek. Similarly, updated information about manufacturers and products is needed in a timely manner. This *Annual Supplement to The Piano Book,* published each summer, is designed to fill that information gap. I hope this modest companion volume will effectively extend the "shelf life" of *The Piano Book* as a valuable reference work, and serve as an additional information resource for piano buyers and piano lovers.

Larry Fine

June, 2002

CONTENTS

MANUFACTURER and PRODUCT UPDATE

This section describes changes to companies, products, and brand names since the fourth edition of *The Piano Book* went to press in the fall of 2000. This section is cumulative; that is, information contained in last year's *Supplement*, to the extent it is still accurate, is repeated here and changes that have occurred during the past year have been added. If a company or brand name is not listed here, it means that there is nothing new of substance to report.

It is not intended, of course, that the information in this update section take the place of the reviews in *The Piano Book*. With some exceptions, the update is limited to changes of a factual nature only, whereas the main book contains, in addition, critical reviews, ratings, and recommendations. Readers should understand that, in most cases, changes in the quality of any particular brand of piano occur very slowly, over a period of many years, if at all. Only where there has been an abrupt change in company ownership, or a period of rapid technological or economic change in the country of origin, is there likely to be a change in quality worth worrying about. For that reason, the reviews in *The Piano Book* can still be considered reliable unless otherwise noted here.

Trends

Pianos made in China continue to improve and make inroads into the North American market. As of last year, several makers had succeeded in producing pianos that were technically acceptable, but few were musically desirable. This year the musical qualities have taken a big leap forward. Special mention in this regard goes to the vertical pianos from the Yantai Longfeng factory, sold here under the Kingsburg and Gebr. Perzina labels, and the grands from Dongbei, sold under the names Nordiska, Everett, and Story & Clark, among others. The jury is still out as to whether these pianos will hold up over the long term and in demanding climates and situations. So far, though, reports on most of them are encouraging. At least as short-term investments, and in milder climates and less demanding situations, they are probably okay.

On the other end of the price spectrum, European piano makers seem to be in a race to redesign their pianos for better sound projection and sustain, à la Steinway. The European piano market is dead, the U.S. market for high-end pianos is—relatively speaking—thriving, and for a number of companies, Steinway is the principal competitor. Considering how tradition-bound these companies are, this degree of activity is unusual. Some of the redesigns—new models from Seiler and Schimmel come to mind—have been terrific musical successes. My only worry is that the palette of available piano tonal qualities is becoming smaller and more homogeneous as the old-world sounds pass away.

ALTENBURG

Correction to web site address: www.altenburgpiano.com

ASTIN-WEIGHT

Correction to web site address: astin-weightpianos.uswestdex.com
(Note: Do not begin with "www".)

New e-mail address: gr8pianos@networld.com

BACHENDORFF (new listing)

Keyboard Distributors Inc.
2512 Palm Ridge
Las Vegas, Nevada 89134

866-469-2224
bachendorffpianos@hotmail.com
www.bachendorffpianos.com

Pianos made by: Daewoo, Kyungki-do, South Korea

These are the Korean-made Ibach pianos described under "Ibach" in *The Piano Book*. They are now being distributed in the U.S. under the Bachendorff name.

With regard to particular model designations, the "RC" models have Renner actions and, for the most part, traditional styling. The letter "S" at the end of the model indicates a straight leg, "A" a curved leg. Models beginning with "C" are decorator-style models without Renner actions. Models 115SE and 115AE are styled like the RC models, but without Renner actions. A Renner action can be added for an additional $1,200.

BALDWIN
including Chickering and Wurlitzer

New address, phone, and ownership:

Baldwin Piano Company
309 Plus Park Blvd.
Nashville, Tennessee 37217

615-871-4500

Owned by: Gibson Piano Ventures, a wholly owned subsidiary of Gibson Guitar Corp.

Shortly after the fourth edition of *The Piano Book* was published in early 2001, the Baldwin board of directors hired a new management team to try to stave off impending bankruptcy caused by a series of costly mistakes and prior poor management. Avoiding bankruptcy turned out not to be possible, and the company filed for protection under Chapter 11 of the U.S. bankruptcy laws in May of 2001. On October 16, 2001, Baldwin's major creditor, General Electric Capital, purchased the company's assets at a court-ordered liquidation sale and then sold them to the Gibson Guitar Corp. on November 9, 2001.

Gibson owners Henry Juszkiewicz and Dave Berryman purchased Gibson in 1986 when it was in complete disarray and turned it into an extremely profitable and well-respected company. They feel that there are many parallels between Gibson's situation at that time and Baldwin's present situation, and expect to be able to turn Baldwin around as well.

Baldwin's new owners say they plan to make large capital investments to improve product quality. In addition they are reorganizing the Baldwin factories in Arkansas to once again produce grands in Conway and verticals in Trumann. This will result in the rehiring of many skilled workers who had been laid off when prior management consolidated most Baldwin manufacturing in the Trumann plant. The Juarez, Mexico action-making facility will also be reopened. A woodworking plant in Greenwood, Mississippi closed in mid-2000 will have its functions transferred to a new woodworking plant in Trumann for increased efficiency. A great cost savings will be realized by the transfer of all Baldwin sales, marketing, and administrative functions to Gibson headquarters in Nashville. Baldwin's line of digital pianos will be discontinued for the time being.

Prior to the management reorganization and subsequent bankruptcy, Baldwin had announced a number of changes to its product line. These changes were never fully realized due to the bankruptcy. For the time being, Baldwin's new owners plan to complete implementation of these changes, described below, but further changes are to be expected as Baldwin's reorganization evolves.

The model E-100 console has been discontinued and replaced with a continental or Eurostyle studio without legs, 44" model E-101. The model E250 Hamilton studio in polyester finish has been discontinued. (The other Hamilton studios remain.)

In the grands, the new model 225E is the model M (5' 2") in French Provincial styling. The 7' model SF-10 has been renamed SF-10E in honor of its adoption of the enhanced features of the upgraded Artist series grands (see *The Piano Book* for details).

The Chickering grands reported on in *The Piano Book* have been withdrawn and replaced by three new pianos—5' 4", 5' 9", and 6' 2"—in fourteen different models in five furniture styles. The plates and cabinets include some features taken from old Chickering designs. These models are the latest in a long series of joint ventures between Baldwin and Samick, and are made in the Samick factories in Korea. In my estimation, the quality should be much better than the Chickerings being withdrawn, probably comparable to other Samick-made instruments.

When Gibson acquired Baldwin, it acquired only its assets, not its liabilities. Therefore, the company is not required to honor warranty claims for pianos purchased prior to the acquisition date. Pianos purchased by the consumer on or after November 9, 2001 are eligible for warranty coverage, even if the dealer purchased the piano before that date. Warranty coverage for pianos purchased by the consumer before November 9, 2001 will only be considered on a case-by-case basis.

In mid-April 2002, Baldwin cancelled agreements with most of its dealers, retaining only the most active ones. The company says it intends to rebuild its dealer network, inviting new dealers to demonstrate their commitment, in part by making large purchases from the company. Baldwin says, however, that it *will* honor the warranty on pianos purchased from "cancelled" dealers, even though, technically, they are no longer "authorized" dealers.

Gibson appears to have a reasonable chance to turn Baldwin around. The company also has a good track record with regard to continued ownership of other acquired companies and the honoring of their warranties. Nevertheless, such undertakings are obviously not without risk. Therefore, I would advise purchasers of Baldwin products to obtain a written warranty from the dealer covering parts and labor for at least ten years in addition to whatever manufacturer's warranty may come with the product.

BECHSTEIN, C.

Web site address: www.bechstein.de

The 9' 2" model D-280 concert grand has been redesigned, with a capo bar and duplex scale in the treble for better tonal projection. Also, unlike most other Bechsteins, which utilize an open pinblock design, this concert grand plate covers the pinblock area. These features have also been added to the 6' 2" model A-189 grand.

Bechstein has introduced a new series of very beautiful designer verticals called "ProBechstein" in 45½", 46½", and 49" sizes. In the pricing guide section, they are the models called "Balance," "Advance," and "Ars Nova."

In late 2002 or early 2003, Bechstein will be introducing two new grands into the American market: 6' 5" model M-192, and 7' model B-210.

For information about changes to the W. Hoffmann line of pianos, see in this section under "Hoffmann, W."

BECKER, J.

All J. Becker verticals now feature agraffes throughout the scale.

BERGMANN

See "Young Chang"

BLONDEL, G.

Distribution of Blondel pianos in the U.S. has been discontinued.

BLÜTHNER

In honor of the company's 150th anniversary, Blüthner has introduced a Jubilee model which has a commemorative cast-iron plate in the style of the special-edition pianos of a century ago. Any grand piano model can be special-ordered with this commemorative plate.

In what is perhaps a world's "first," Blüthner has designed and built a piano for left-handed pianists. This is a completely "backwards" piano, with the treble keys, hammers, and strings on the left and the bass on the right. When it was introduced, a pianist gave a concert on it after only a couple of hours of practice! It is currently available in the 6' 10" and 9' 2" sizes by special order (price not available).

BÖSENDORFER

New U.S. distributor address, phone, and e-mail:

Bösendorfer USA
577B Hackman Road
Lititz, Pennsylvania 17543

888-936-2516
bosendorferusa@aol.com

In January 2002, Bösendorfer was purchased from Kimball International by the BAWAG - P.S.K. Group, Austria's third largest banking group. Bösendorfer has a special place in Austrian history and culture, and although the company has thrived under Kimball's ownership, for some time there has been a desire on all sides to return Bösendorfer to Austrian hands. The new owner says it intends to maintain the same high standards of material and workmanship for which the company is renowned. It will also continue the new marketing course of the last few years, including the redesign of existing models, a new "Artisan" series of art case pianos, and the Conservatory series of cosmetically reduced, less expensive versions of its models.

In 2001, Bösendorfer introduced a new 9' 2" model 280 concert grand, and in 2002, a 6' 2" model 185 grand. These and other new and redesigned models share a new design philosophy in which the treble soundboard area is increased for better tonal projection by reducing excess cabinet distance between player and strings, and the bass soundboard area is increased for better bass response by joining the wide tail to the spine at a sharper corner.

The new concert grand is in addition to the two other concert grands (9' and 9' 6") the company already produces. Unlike the others, however, which have 92 and 97 keys, respectively, this new model has only 88 keys. Its scale design also features a front duplex and new action geometry. The company says the new model is intended for concert pianists who would otherwise be distracted or intimidated by the presence of additional keys in the bass. To my ears, the new piano has better sustain in the treble than I usually find in Bösendorfer pianos, but otherwise has a characteristic Bösendorfer sound and feel. The 9' model 275 is now available only by special order.

BOSTON

The 49" vertical model UP-125 has been replaced with a completely redesigned 50" model UP-126. In the redesign, the wooden back has been made much heftier and the plate much more rigid to better resist torsional and bending stresses. The bass scale has been reworked with reduced string tension for smoother bass tone, and the soundboard taper and rib placement have been refined for better treble tone. Lastly, the music desk for the European-style case design has been improved so that it holds music more securely. Similar changes are scheduled for the 52" model.

THE BRITISH PIANO MANUFACTURING COMPANY LTD.
(new listing)

The British Piano Manufacturing Co. Ltd.
Woodchester Mills
Woodchester, Stroud,
Glos. GL5 5NW England

(44) 1453-872871
bpmc@woodchestermill.fsbusiness.co.uk
www.pianoforte.co.uk

This is the new name, address, and phone number for the company formerly known as Whelpdale, Maxwell & Codd. This company produces Welmar, Knight, Broadwood, Bentley, and now Woodchester pianos. It purchased Woodchester last year and moved the manufacturing facilities for all its brands to the Woodchester factory, formerly the Bentley factory (see *The Piano Book* for history). However, the U.S. contact for Woodchester (only) remains unchanged (see *The Piano Book* under "Woodchester").

Clarification: In *The Piano Book* entry for Whelpdale Maxwell & Codd, I wrote that John Broadwood & Sons was established in 1728. It has been brought to my attention that this is not possible because Broadwood was not born until 1732. The 1728 (or 1729) date is widely used, however, and it probably represents the date of establishment of the shop of Burkat Shudi, with whom Broadwood apprenticed (1761), and of whose business Broadwood later became partner (1770) and, eventually, sole proprietor (1782).

CHICKERING

See "Baldwin"

DISKLAVIER

See "Yamaha"

EISENBERG

See "Steinberg, Wilh."

ESSEX

Steinway, through its Boston Piano Co. subsidiary, introduced several "Essex" models in early 2001 and 2002. These are manufactured in Korea by Young Chang. They include 5' 3" and 6' grands and 42", 44", and 48" verticals. The 42" and 44" vertical models are of identical scale design, but the smaller one is in a continental-style cabinet. Some of the vertical cabinets look backward to styles of past decades of the twentieth century. The grands are in Art Deco style. At press time, only the ebony versions of the 6' grand had been announced. It is expected, however, that this model will eventually be available in the same finishes as the 5' 3" model.

Steinway says that it designed these pianos using state-of-the-art structural analysis software similar to that used in the auto and aircraft industries, allowing it to test the effects of a large number of variables in a short amount of time without having to build innumerable prototypes. Like Boston pianos, the Essex line was designed with a lower tension duplex scale and a larger, tapered solid spruce soundboard, for potentially better sustain. The grands utilize rosette-shaped flanges for better action stability.

ESTONIA

Technicians report that Estonia pianos are now arriving at the dealer better prepared, and seem not to have problems anymore with uneven tuning pin tightness.

FAZIOLI

Corrections to review: Three lids are optional on the 10' 2" grand. The 5' 2" and 6' models utilize a Delignit pinblock as mentioned, but the larger models have Bolduc (Canadian) pinblocks. The Fazioli warranty has been increased to ten years.

Additional web site address: www.fazioli.com

FEURICH

U.S. contact:

Warfield Piano
821 Kent Avenue
Baltimore, Maryland 21228

410-747-7700
TheWarfield@earthlink.net
www.feurich.com

Pianos made by: Feurich Klavier-u.Flügelfabrikation GmbH, Gunzenhausen, Germany

This venerable German manufacturer is once again making pianos in its own factory. The models being offered at this time are 46½" (F118) and 48½" (F123) verticals and 5' 8" (F172) and 7' 5" (F227) grands. A 45½" model F116 is the same as the F118, but without casters, and model F117 is the same as the F118, but in a simpler cabinet.

FÖRSTER, AUGUST

New web site address: www.august-foerster.de

GROTRIAN

Grotrian has introduced the Duo Grand Piano, two grand pianos placed side by side with keyboards at opposite ends, as in a duo piano concert, with removable rim parts, connected soundboards, and a common lid (price not yet available).

HALLET, DAVIS & CO.

Some of the Chinese-made Hallet & Davis pianos are now being made by the Dongbei Piano Co.

HEINTZMAN

The assets of the Heintzman piano company were purchased by a Chinese company and moved from Canada to Beijing, where pianos are now produced under that name by a firm known as Beijing Heintzman. This factory has some investment by the Beijing Xinghai Piano Co., but is a separate venture at a separate location. Prices were not available at press time. Although information about these pianos is scarce, my sources tell me that the quality is a little higher than that of some of the other Beijing-made pianos. See also "Xinghai / Otto Meister".

HOFFMANN, W.

W. Hoffmann pianos now are separated into two types: the Standard Series and the Conservatory Series.

The Standard Series consists of the 5' 2" and 6' 1" grands and the 48", 49", and 52" verticals. These pianos are made entirely at the Bohemia factory in the Czech Republic. Unlike the pianos until recently assembled there with Young Chang parts and sold under the Rieger-Kloss name (now discontinued), the W. Hoffmann pianos are made almost entirely of Czech parts with considerable input from Bechstein's design and engineering departments. The grands and the 52" vertical have Renner actions.

The Conservatory Series consists of the new 6' 3" grand, and the 46", 47", and 50" verticals with model designations marked "Trend". The grand is designed and engineered by Bechstein, but some of the assembly work is done in other European factories under Bechstein's supervision. It uses all Bechstein parts with a Renner action. The Trend models, as before, are made entirely at the Bechstein factory in Seifhennersdorf, Germany.

HOFMANN & SCHOLZ / MECKLENBURG

This company says it now has its own key-making facilities.

A new 6' 1" model 183 has been introduced. It is made for the company at the Niendorf factory.

IBACH

The Ibach-Daewoo joint venture mentioned in *The Piano Book* was sold by Daewoo to a music industry investment group called Veloce Ltd. The Korean-made pianos are being distributed in the U.S. under the name Bachendorff and in Canada under the name Royale. See "Bachendorff" for more information about the U.S.-distributed pianos.

KAWAI

Additional web site address: www.shigerukawai.com

Kawai has opened a factory in Indonesia, where it will be making cabinets and back assemblies for some vertical piano models sold in the U.S., as well as in other parts of the world. Kawai also produces several vertical models in joint venture with the Beijing Xinghai Piano Co. in China. These pianos are sold in Canada and Europe, but not in the U.S. At one time these pianos bore the name "Linden", but use of that name has been discontinued.

True to its reputation, Kawai has made even more changes to its product line. The model 505 and 605 furniture-style consoles have been discontinued and replaced with several 44½" and 45" models utilizing the same scale design as the 605. Model 506S is this piano in a simple, Indonesian-made studio-style cabinet. Although called a "studio" because of the cabinet style, it has a compressed action characteristic of a console. Model 606 is this piano in a furniture-style console and comes in two levels of cabinetry, the more expensive ones having inlayed veneers. Model K-18 is the 506S in a Japanese-style, polyester-finished cabinet. It replaces the recent CX-10 and its predecessor, the popular model CX-5H, as Kawai's low-priced "studio." The 46½" furniture-style studio model 902 has been changed to model 906, with a stiffer back structure, all ABS action parts, and new cabinetry. Models K-22 (satin ebony) and K-25 (polished ebony) are like the 48" model K-30, except in a simpler cabinet. UST-10 is the K-30 in an institutional (school) cabinet.

In the grands, the 5' model GM-2A has become model GM-10. The 5' 1" model GE-1A has been replaced by the GE-20, which has the features of the former GE-1AS model. A new 5' 5" model GE-30 has been introduced. It has the same scale as the model RX-1, but is like the other GE models structurally and in terms of its features (see *The Piano Book* for details on the differences between the RX, GE, and GM models). The Shigeru Kawai pianos are now available in six different models from 5' 10" to 9' 1".

KEMBLE

New U.S. distributor:

Poppenberg & Associates
966 South Pearl Street
Denver, Colorado 80209

303-765-5775

The "Cambridge" models have been discontinued. A new 46½" "Windsor" model has been added. This model has a fancier cabinet and a more powerful bass than the 45" "Traditional" model. The 52" vertical, formerly available only as a limited-edition designer model, is now available as a regular model.

KINGSBURG

Although a U.S. distributor for Kingsburg is listed in *The Piano Book*, an additional distributor is:

Piano Empire, Inc.
13370 E. Firestone Blvd., Ste. A
Santa Fe Springs, CA 90670

800-576-3463
562-926-1906
info@kingsburgpiano.com
www.kingsburgpiano.com

There is a new 4' 11" model F-150 grand.

See also "Perzina, Gebr." in this section.

KNABE, WM.

See under "Samick" in this section.

KRAKAUER

New e-mail address: daguillaume@earthlink.net

MASON & HAMLIN

Mason & Hamlin is working on a new 6' 3" model AA grand, to be introduced in 2002 or 2003.

MEISTER, OTTO

See under "Xinghai / Otto Meister"

MILLER, HENRY F.

This is the name of an old American piano maker, no longer in business. The name is now owned by the Sherman Clay chain of piano stores. The pianos are made by Pearl River in China and are similar to pianos sold under the

Pearl River name. They are sold primarily in Sherman Clay and Jordan Kitt's piano stores, as well as a few others.

NORDISKA

There is a new 50" model 126 vertical piano, with six full-length spruce backposts and Abel hammers, among other features.

PEARL RIVER

New address and phone number for U.S. distributor:

Pearl River Piano Group America, Ltd.
1521 South Carlos Avenue
Ontario, California 91761

909-673-9155
800-435-5086
www.pearlriverpianos.com

Pearl River has added a 6' 4" grand to its regular line and a 49" vertical model 126R to its Ritmüller line. The vertical is based on the model 125M1 joint venture piano, but with agraffes throughout the scale. The 7' and 9' Pearl River grands now come with Renner actions.

Correction: The 4' 7" Ritmüller grand does not have a Renner action.

PERZINA, GEBR. (new listing)

Piano Empire, Inc.
13370 E. Firestone Blvd., Ste. A
Santa Fe Springs, CA 90670

800-576-3463
562-926-1906
info@kingsburgpiano.com
www.kingsburgpiano.com

Pianos made by: Yantai Longfeng Piano Co., Ltd., Yantai, China

The Gebr. Perzina piano company was established in the German town of Schwerin in 1871, and was a prominent piano maker until World War I, after which its fortunes declined. In more recent times, the factory was moved to the nearby city of Lenzen and the company is now known as Pianofabrik Lenzen GmbH. In the early 1990s, the company was purchased by Music Brokers International B.V. in The Netherlands. Eventually it was decided that making pianos in Germany was not economically viable, so manufacturing was moved to Yantai, China, where 47", 48", and 51" verticals are being made by the Yantai Longfeng Piano Co., the same company that makes Kingsburg pianos. (See also under "Kingsburg" in *The Piano Book* and this *Supplement*.)

Lenzen says it ships many European materials to Yantai, including Roslau strings, Delignit pinblocks, English felts, and European veneers, as well as Alaskan Sitka spruce. New machinery is from Japan and Italy. According to the company, all the piano designs are the original German scales. One of the notable features of the vertical piano is its "floating" soundboard design. The soundboard is unattached to the back at certain points for freer vibration.

PETROF

Web site address: www.petrof.com

Petrof has introduced a new concert grand called the "P1 Mistral." The company says the instrument utilizes a more rigid brace and frame, front and rear duplex scales, and a Renner action, among other features. The Magnetic Balanced Action feature (see page 233 of *The Piano Book*) is available as an option. Also new is a 53" vertical model P135. It has a Renner action, full sostenuto, a soft-close fallboard, and a newly-designed adjustable music desk, among other features.

PIANODISC

PianoDisc has replaced the PDS 128 Plus system with the 228 CFX. The main difference is that the 228 CFX has both a floppy drive and a CD drive as standard equipment, so it is unnecessary to plug in your own CD player (although you can do so if you have a multi-disc CD changer you want to use). The company says that the control box is the smallest such box with both floppy and CD drives on the market. It can be mounted on the piano or can be located up to 100 feet away and operated with the included infrared wireless remote control.

PianoDisc has introduced an MX Platinum option that utilizes 64 MB of flash memory to store hours of music and play it back without ever having to change a disk. MX Platinum comes with 35 hours of pre-selected music (589 songs), to which one can add music from floppy disks, TFT MIDI

Record, and standard MIDI files (but not PianoDisc CDs). PianoDisc's regular MX feature with 32 MB of flash memory still remains available as an option.

The GT360 and GT90 QuietTime systems have been discontinued and replaced with a QuietTime system that includes most of the same components, but without the sound card and control box. The new system comes with a power supply, MIDI cable, a MIDI strip for installing under the keys, three pedal switches, a MIDI board with cover, headphones, and a mute rail that, when activated, prevents the hammers from hitting the strings. Customers can buy and use any off-the-shelf sound module with the system.

PianoDisc has introduced a new remote control called the PianoDisc Home Theater Master. It features an LCD touch screen and eliminates the need to have multiple remote controls to operate other various electronic devices. This remote is specially programmed to operate the PianoDisc and can be programmed to control eleven other Audio and Video components including: Stereo, CD, Tape, CATV, Satellite, TV, DVD, VCR and Laser Disc.

Note Release Control (NRC) has been developed by PianoDisc to reduce noise made by the keys when they are released. This is achieved by pulsing the solenoid during key release to slow the key down. This new feature is compatible with all PDS 128+ and 228CFX Silent Drive systems, and is added by using the Flash Memory feature that allows for convenient software upgrades. To add NRC at no charge, get the PianoDisc Update 4.2 and Silent Drive CPU Update F from the PianoDisc web site or from an authorized PianoDisc installer.

PLEYEL

Web site address: www.pleyel.fr

Pleyel has introduced a new 5' 8" model 170 grand piano.

PRAMBERGER

See "Young Chang"

QRS / PIANOMATION

QRS has acquired the exclusive rights to manufacture and sell a Self-Tuning Piano System (which does not yet have a trade name). The company says the system will be designed into the manufacture of a piano and will allow the piano to maintain itself in tune electronically or to be tuned before each use by simply turning on a switch. Except to say that it involves no motors or moving parts, the company has not yet divulged how the system accomplishes this task. The system was invented by Don A. Gilmore of Kansas City, Missouri. QRS expects the system to be available in the fall of 2002.

RIDGEWOOD

The Ridgewood and Sagenhaft names are now applied interchangeably at dealer request to three models of piano from the Dongbei Piano Co., the model 112 vertical and the 5' and 5' 5" grands. All other Ridgewood and Sagenhaft models have been discontinued. For prices, see under "Sagenhaft/Ridgewood" in the Pricing Guide section.

RIEGER-KLOSS

The Rieger-Kloss line of pianos has been discontinued. The Bohemia Piano Co. is now making pianos for Bechstein under the W. Hoffmann name. See under "Hoffmann, W." in this section for more information.

RITMÜLLER

See under "Pearl River".

SAGENHAFT

The Ridgewood and Sagenhaft names are now applied interchangeably at dealer request to three models of piano from the Dongbei Piano Co., the model 112 vertical and the 5' and 5' 5" grands. All other Ridgewood and Sagenhaft models have been discontinued.

SAMICK

The Knabe piano line made by Young Chang for PianoDisc has been discontinued, and the name has been sold to Samick. Samick is now using this name on the pianos formerly sold as the "World Piano" premium line of Samick pianos (see *The Piano Book* for details). Samick says plans are underway to make a new premium-level piano with the Knabe name based on the original Knabe scale designs and cabinet styles, with sand-cast plates and lacquer finishes. Knabe prices were not available at press time.

Samick has discontinued a number of models in both its Samick and Kohler & Campbell lines and has come out with some new ones as well, both Korean and Indonesian. In general, it is continuing its trend of moving much of its production to Indonesia, while concentrating its Korean production on higher-end models.

SAUTER

Additional web site address: www.sauter-pianos.de

Sauter has introduced a new 44" model 112 with adjustable feet for leveling the piano or for making the piano fit securely on an unlevel floor. There is also a quite beautiful new Peter Maly–designed version of the 48" model with butterfly lids.

SCHIMMEL

New address for U.S. distributor:

Schimmel Piano Corporation
577B Hackman Road
Lititz, Pennsylvania 17543

Schimmel has developed several new upright models based on a more traditional philosphy of construction. These are the F 122 (48"), S 125 (49"), and O 132 (52"). Older models in the same or similar sizes continue to be produced, however. In the older models, the plate is the main structural support and contains a pocket for the pinblock. In the new models, traditional back posts assume a greater role for support, and the pinblock and soundboard are attached to the posts. The company says that the joining of wooden structural and acoustical parts enhances the tone. The new models also incorporate duplex scaling.

Schimmel has released a new 5' 7" model 169 grand. The company says the piano has the same treble scale and action as its 7' grand, and almost the same size soundboard as its 6' grand. To obtain the larger soundboard, the case sides are angled slightly. The soundboard and ribs were also modified for tonal improvement. This philosophy of marrying the front end of the 7' grand to other sizes of piano is one that Schimmel plans to extend to other models as it creates a "family" of redesigned grands. An example of the new 5' 7" grand I played was typically bright, but had very good sustain and the feel of a larger piano. I was impressed with it.

SCHULZE POLLMANN

Schulze Pollmann has introduced a new 5' 3" model 160 grand. It comes with a Detoa action, but can be ordered with a Renner action at additional cost. The 46" model 117 vertical has a new scale design with agraffes and has been redesignated as model 118/P8. The 50" model 126E has been similarly redesigned and is now called 126P6.

SEILER

New U.S. contact information for Seiler:

Don Stephenson
Seiler Piano
7188 North Bergen Road
Bergen, New York 14416

888-621-1137
america@seiler-pianos.com
www.seiler-pianos.com

Grand model 206 has been redesigned and is now 6' 10" model 208 with a duplex scale, longer strings, larger soundboard area, longer keys, and a lighter touch. Model 240 as been redesigned with the same changes and is now 8' 1" model 242. Musically, both of these redesigned models are very successful. They retain the typical Seiler clarity, but with longer sustain and a marvelously even-feeling touch — a real pleasure to play.

Seiler says that if there is no Seiler dealer in the customer's area, the customer can contact the U.S. representative to arrange for a direct purchase from Germany.

Correction: Seiler makes approximately 2,000 pianos a year.

SHERMAN CLAY

Correction: I have been told that for much of the 1970s and 1980s, pianos sold under the Sherman Clay label were made by Kimball or Aeolian. In the mid to late 1980s, some Sherman Clay pianos were made by Daewoo (Sojin).

STECK, GEORGE

PianoDisc has discontinued its George Steck line of PianoDisc-equipped, Chinese-made pianos. No plans have yet been made for the name's future use.

STEINBERG, WILH.

The name of the manufacturer has changed from Wilhelm Steinberg Pianofortefabrik Gmbh to Thüringer Pianoforte GmbH. The company has also sold its key-making business to Kluge, now part of Steinway.

A new 48" model C2 vertical has a simpler cabinet than the company's IQ models. Steinberg says it will not be making the 49" vertical available with a Fandrich action, as mentioned in *The Piano Book*.

The warranty has been changed to five years, parts and labor.

Correction: *The Piano Book* says that the Wilh. Steinberg grand is identical to the Steingraeber grand. Although the Steinberg grand evolved from the Steingraeber, unlike the Steingraeber, the Steinberg has a duplex scale, as well as a different method of rim construction and a different bridge design.

"Eisenberg" is a new, lower-priced line from Steinberg, made in cooperation with other European factories. Prices and models are not yet firm.

STEINER, BERNHARD

Web site address: www.bernhardsteiner.com

STEINGRAEBER & SÖHNE

Additional web site address: www.steingraeber.de

Steingraeber has a new 8' 9" concert grand, model E-272 (price not available).

Steingraeber is known for its many innovative technical improvements to the piano. The newest one is a cylindrical knuckle (grand piano part) that revolves when played softly. It acts like a normal knuckle during normal and hard playing, but the revolving knuckle makes pianissimo playing easier, smoother, and more accurate.

STEINWAY & SONS

Steinway has launched its new Legendary Collection—one-of-a-kind reproductions of historical art case pianos—with a reproduction of the famous Alma Tadema art case Steinway. Commissioned in the 1880s by Henry Marquand, then-president of the Metropolitan Museum of Art in New York, this piano was designed and created by the famous English design firm of Sir Lawrence Alma-Tadema. In 1997, it was purchased at Sotheby's for $1,200,000. Offered at a price of $675,000, the reproduction, like the original, contains just about every possible art case decoration possible, including elaborate carvings, 17 different levels of decorative moldings, medallions, engravings, inlaid mother-of-pearl, marquetry, goatskin parchment, a frieze consisting of more than 6,000 parts, and even an oil painting. It is considered the most expensive piano ever built.

Correction: On page 206 of *The Piano Book*, I wrote that Steinway operated its own plate foundry until about 1930. My sources now tell me that the foundry operated until about 1939 or 1940.

STORY & CLARK

Web site address: www.storyandclark.com

In part due to economic factors and in part because of the problems of Baldwin, a principal supplier of parts, Story & Clark has ceased all its U.S. piano production. Pianos bearing the Story & Clark name are now made in China by the Dongbei and Beijing piano companies.

STRAUSS

Web site address: www.strausspiano.com

A new 46½" model UP-118 vertical I saw at a trade show sounded, played, and looked much better than previous models I have seen from this company.

The company now provides a ten year limited parts and labor warranty from the manufacturer.

WALTER, CHARLES R.

Web site address: walterpiano.com

Walter says he has made some changes to his vertical pianos to better control tuning pin torque (tightness), to reduce the incidence of false beats in the treble, and to smooth out the break between tenor and bass.

WEBER

Weber has introduced a number of "special edition" grand and vertical models. The "WSG" grand models—5' 1", 5' 7", and 6' 1"—have tapered soundboards, "best quality" Young Chang actions, and cosmetic enhancements. The "WSF" and "WSE" 43½" and 48" verticals have cosmetic and action enhancements and the 43½" has a slow-fall fallboard.

Weber has added two more Chinese-made grands to its line, 5' 2" and 5' 9". These are made in Young Chang's Tianjin factory.

WHELPDALE, MAXWELL & CODD

This company has been renamed The British Piano Manufacturing Company Ltd. See under that name for more information.

WOODCHESTER

Additional web site address: www.uk-piano.org/woodchester

Woodchester has been purchased by Whelpdale, Maxwell & Codd, now called The British Piano Manufacturing Company Ltd. See under that name for more information. However, the U.S. contact for Woodchester remains the same as before.

XINGHAI / OTTO MEISTER (new listing)

These brands are made by the Beijing Xinghai Piano Co. in China. No further information is available. See also "Heintzman".

YAMAHA
including Disklavier

Yamaha is selling a less expensive, Indonesian-made version of its 4' 11" model GA1 grand, the model GA1E. The Japanese-made GA1 version is now available only as a Disklavier model DGA1.

Perhaps in response to criticisms of the tone of its 5' 3" GH1B series of grands (or perhaps because the introduction of an inexpensive piano from Indonesia has made the low-priced 5' 3" pianos redundant), Yamaha has replaced the GH1B series, and the less-expensive variant model GP1, with a new 5' 3" GC1 series. The new models feature the same scale design, duplex scaling, and tone collector construction as the more expensive C1 series, but with a bass sustain pedal instead of a sostenuto, and with less expensive cabinetry and plate finish. The price of the GC1 is about the same as the GH1B and it is available in most of the same furniture styles and finishes. For the time being, only the French Provincial Cherry and Georgian Mahogany versions of the GH1B will continue to be made, as those styles are not yet available in the GC1 line. A Disklavier version of the GC1, the DGC1A, replaces the corresponding Disklavier versions of the GH1B and GP1 pianos being discontinued.

Grand model C3 and its Disklavier counterpart DC3A are now available in a "NEO" cabinet style—a modernistic case with an acrylic lid, silver plate, and cherry legs. The model C1 "Metro" and its Disklavier counterpart are special centennial edition pianos with a unique rim design in polished ebony and champagne gold. They mark the 100th anniversary of the first Yamaha grand.

Fancy furniture versions of the popular P22 studio will be offered beginning in fall 2002 as model P600. Prices were not yet available at press time. Upright models U1 and U3 now sport a longer music desk—a very welcome addition. Model U3 joins model U5 in the use of a "floating" soundboard support system—the soundboard is not completely attached to the back at the top, allowing it to vibrate a little more freely for enhanced tonal performance.

The "A" at the end of most Disklavier model designations refers to the new CD (audio) function in these instruments, one of the Mark III (i.e., third generation) Disklavier features. Disklavier grands are no longer available without the CD function, except for model DGA1. Most Disklavier verticals don't have the CD function; however, it can be added. DCD1 is an add-on CD drive that can be added to any Disklavier grand or vertical, new or old.

The model DU1A will be a new Disklavier version of the 48" U1 upright. It will be the only Disklavier upright with Mark III features. It will replace both the MX1Z Disklavier and the MPX1Z Disklavier with Silent Feature. The DU1A will contain the Silent Feature; a version of this model without the Silent Feature will no longer be offered. Prices were not yet available at press time, but are expected to be slightly higher than those for the MPX1Z. The 48" MIDIPiano model MP1Z will become the MPU1.

Disklavier Pro models now have all the Mark III Disklavier features (except built-in speakers), including the CD drive, 16 MB of flash memory, and SmartKey and CueTime.

PianoSmart technology is a new feature of all Mark III Disklavier pianos. Yamaha has prepared a piano track in MIDI format on a floppy disk to go along with each of a number of popular audio CDs available on the general market. When the owner plays both the floppy and the CD at the same time, PianoSmart links them together, enabling the Disklavier to accurately play along with the CD. One can also record a piano accompaniment to a favorite audio CD. Pop the CD and a blank floppy into a Mark III Disklavier and record yourself playing along. The two will then be linked together for future playback. PianoSmart is available as a free software upgrade from Yamaha. The "smart" MIDI files will be added to the library of Disklavier musical offerings available from Yamaha.

YOUNG CHANG
including Bergmann and Pramberger

Young Chang says it has changed the front duplex scale on all its grand models to a new configuration for a cleaner sound.

All Bergmann model numbers now begin with "B," the grands with "BTG." A new 5' 9" model BTG-175 and 6' 1" model BTG-185, both made in China, are based on the scales of the corresponding Young Chang "Gold" series pianos from Korea. A new 43" model BAF-110 is the model BAF-108 with a nicer cabinet.

Additions to the Pramberger "Platinum Edition" series now includes a 52" model JP-52 upright and a 7' 6" model JP-228 grand.

MODEL and PRICING GUIDE

This guide contains the "list price" for nearly every brand, model, style, and finish of new piano that has regular distribution in the United States and, for the most part, Canada. Some marginal, local, or "stencil" brands are omitted. Except where indicated, prices are in U.S. dollars and the pianos are assumed to be for sale in the U.S. (Canadians will find the information useful after translation into Canadian dollars, but there may be differences in import duties and sales practices that will affect retail prices.) Prices and specifications are, of course, subject to change. Most manufacturers revise their prices at least once a year; two or three times a year is not uncommon when currency exchange rates are unstable. The prices in this edition were compiled in the spring of 2002.

Some terms used in this guide require special explanation and disclaimers:

List Price

The list price is usually a starting point for negotiation, not a final sales price. The term "list price," as used in this *Supplement*, is a "standard" list price computed from the published wholesale price according to a formula commonly used in the industry. Some manufacturers use a different formula, however, for their own suggested retail prices, usually one that raises the prices above "standard" list by ten to fifteen percent so that their dealers can advertise a larger "discount" without losing profit. For this reason, price-shopping by comparing discounts from the manufacturers' own suggested retail prices may result in a faulty price comparison. To provide a level playing field for comparing prices, all prices in this guide are computed according to a uniform "standard" formula, *even though it may differ from the manufacturers' own suggested retail prices.* Where my list prices and those of a manufacturer differ, then, no dishonesty should be inferred; we simply employ different formulas. For most brands, but not all, the price includes a bench and the standard manufacturer's warranty for that brand (see *The Piano Book* for details). Prices for some European brands do not include a bench. Most dealers will also include moving and one or two tunings in the home, but these are optional and a matter of agreement between you and the dealer.

Style and Finish

Unless otherwise indicated, the cabinet style is assumed to be "traditional" and is not stated. Exactly what "traditional" means varies from brand to brand. In general, it is a "classic" styling with minimal embellishment and straight legs. The vertical pianos have front legs, which are free-standing on smaller verticals and attached to the cabinet with toe blocks on larger verticals. "Continental" or European styling refers to vertical pianos without decorative trim and usually without front legs. Other furniture styles (Chippendale, French Provincial, Queen Anne, etc.) are as noted. The manufacturer's own trademarked style name is used when an appropriate generic name could not be determined.

Unless otherwise stated, all finishes are assumed to be "satin," which reflects light but not images. "Polished" finishes, also known as "high-gloss" or "high-polish," are mirror-like. "Oiled" finishes are usually matte (not shiny). "Open-pore" finishes, common on some European pianos, are slightly "grainier" satin finishes due to the wood pores not being filled in prior to finishing. In fact, many finishes labeled "satin" on European pianos are actually open-pore. "Ebony" is a black finish.

Special-order–only styles and finishes are in italics.

Some descriptions of style and finish may be slightly different from the manufacturer's own for the purpose of clarity, consistency, saving space, or other reason.

Size

The height of a vertical piano is measured from the floor to the top of the piano. The length of a grand piano is measured from the very front (keyboard end) to the very back (tail end).

About Actual Selling or "Street" Prices

Buying a piano is something like buying a car—the list price is deliberately set high in anticipation of negotiating.[*] But sometimes this is carried to extremes, as when the salesperson reduces the price three times in the first fifteen minutes to barely half the sticker price. In situations like this, the customer, understandably confused, is bound to ask in exasperation, "What is the *real* price of this piano?"

---

[*] A relatively small number of dealers have non-negotiable prices.

Unfortunately, there *is* no "real" price. In theory, the dealer pays a wholesale price and then marks it up by an amount sufficient to cover the overhead and produce a profit. In practice, however, the markup can vary considerably from sale to sale depending on such factors as:

- how long the inventory has been sitting around, racking up finance charges for the dealer

- how much of a discount the dealer received at the wholesale level for buying in quantity or for paying cash

- the dealer's cash flow situation

- the competition in that particular geographic area for a particular brand or type of piano

- special piano sales events taking place in the area

- how the salesperson sizes up your situation and your willingness to pay

- the level of pre- and post-sale service the dealer seeks to provide

- the dealer's other overhead expenses

It's not unusual for one person to pay fifty percent more than another for the same brand and model of piano—sometimes even from the same dealer on the same day! It may seem as if pricing is so chaotic that no advice can be given, but in truth, enough piano sales do fall within a certain range of typical profit margins that some guidance is possible as long as the reader understands the limitations inherent in this kind of advice.

Historically, discounts from "standard" list price have averaged ten or fifteen percent in the piano business. In recent years, however, conditions have changed such that, according to some industry sources, the average discount from list has increased to twenty or twenty-five percent. Essentially, due to growing competition from used pianos and digital pianos, and a decrease in the cultural importance attached to having a piano in the home, there are too many dealers of new pianos chasing after too few consumer dollars. In addition, higher labor costs worldwide and unfavorable international currency values make some brands so expensive in the U.S. that they can only be sold at very large discounts. I think, too, that consumers are becoming more savvy and are shopping around. Unfortunately, the overhead costs of running a traditional piano store are so high that most dealers cannot stay in business if they sell at an average discount from "standard" list price of more than about twenty percent. To survive, dealers are evolving multiple new approaches: becoming more efficient, instituting low-price/high volume strategies, cutting their overhead—sometimes including service—or subsidizing their meager sales of new pianos with used pianos (which command higher profit margins), rentals, rebuilding, and other products and services.

Although the average discount has increased, it is by no means uniform. Some brands dependably bring top dollar; others languish or the price is highly situational. I did consider giving a typical range of "street" prices for each brand and model listed in this volume, but concluded that the task would be too daunting due to the extreme variation that can exist from one situation to another, and because of the political fallout that would likely result from dealers and manufacturers who fear the loss of what little power they still have over aggressive, price-shopping customers. So, for now, I've decided just to give general advice in print. (For those who desire more specific information on "street" prices, I offer additional services, such as private telephone consultations and a Pricing Guide Service on the internet. See my web site, **www.pianobook.com**, for more information.)

It should be clearly understood that the advice given here is based on my own observations, subjective judgment, and general understanding of the piano market, *not* on statistical sales data or scientific analysis. (Brand-by-brand statistical sales data are virtually nonexistent.) This knowledge is the product of discussions with hundreds of customers, dealers, technicians, and industry executives over the years. Other industry observers may come to different conclusions. This rundown of "street" prices won't cover every brand, but should give a rough idea of what to expect and the ability to predict prices for some of the brands not specifically covered. I can't emphasize enough, however, that pricing can be highly situational, dependent on the mix of available products and the ease of comparison shopping in any particular geographic area, as well as on the financial situation of dealer and customer. The following generalizations should prove useful to you, but expect almost anything.

As a general rule of thumb:

- the more expensive the piano, the higher the possible discount

- the more "exclusive" a brand is perceived to be, the less likely head-to-head competition, and therefore the lower the possible discount

- the longer a piano remains unsold, the higher the possible discount

- the more service-intensive the piano, the lower the possible discount

Although discounts from "standard" list price for Japanese and Korean pianos typically start at perhaps fifteen percent, twenty or even thirty percent discounts are not uncommon in a moderately competitive environment, especially if the dealer knows the customer is shopping around. Korean pianos are disadvantaged by the presence in the market of too many different brand names made by the same two companies, driving prices down. Some Korean pianos—particularly Young Chang products—are sold at large discounts (ten percent or more) from the published *wholesale* price to dealers who buy in sufficient quantity or for certain models, a savings the dealers can pass on to the retail customers if they choose to do so or if they must do so to compete. (Many manufacturers do this to some extent or from time to time, but Young Chang seems to have a more consistent policy about it.) The problem for the consumer is that these wholesale discounts are not given out uniformly among dealers, so figuring out an appropriate "street" price for a particular dealer, model, and situation from the price information presented in this *Supplement* could be difficult.

The Boston piano, although manufactured in Japan, is generally viewed as being a little more "exclusive" due to its association with Steinway, so deep discounting is much less likely. Discounts in the range of ten percent or so are common. Baldwin, whose pianos are usually seen as being distinctly different from the Asian products even though they often share common price ranges, also benefits from exceptional name recognition and its historical "made in USA" connection. Discounting is likely to be moderate, in my experience—perhaps fifteen to twenty-five percent. (Note: Due to Baldwin's recent bankruptcy and sale, however, discounting has tended to be larger than usual during the past year.)

Western European instruments tend to be extremely expensive here due to their high quality, the high European cost of doing business, additional middlemen/importers and, sometimes, unfavorable exchange rates. There appear to be two types of dealers of these pianos. One type, specializing in selling higher-quality instruments to a demanding clientele, manages to get top dollar for them despite their high price, with discounts averaging only twenty percent or so. They are not particularly into negotiating. The other type of dealer, probably more numerous, depends for his or her "bread and butter" on consumer-grade pianos and is pleased to make a relatively small profit on the occasional sale of a luxury instrument. Discounts here may well approach thirty to forty percent at times, especially if the piano has gone unsold for an extended period of time. Eastern European brands like Petrof and Estonia are already seen as being a good deal for the money and are more service-intensive for the dealer than those from Western Europe, so expect moderate discounts—perhaps fifteen to twenty-five percent.

At the other end of the price spectrum, most Russian and Chinese pianos are so cheap, and require so much servicing by the dealer, that it's simply not cost-effective to sell them for much less than full list price. However, some dealers do use them as "loss leaders," that is, just to get people into the store, whereupon the customer is sold on a more expensive piano. In that situation, the occasional customer who actually chooses to buy the "leader" may do so at a large discount.

Steinway pianos have always been in a class by themselves, historically the only expensive piano to continually command high profit margins. Except for older Steinways and the occasional Mason & Hamlin, Steinway has little competition and fewer than one hundred dealers in the United States. Service requirements can be quite high, at least in part because of the higher standards often required to satisfy a fussier clientele. Historically, Steinway pianos have sold at or near full list price. (Some dealers even sell *above* list!) This is still true in many places, but in recent years I have seen a little more discounting than in the past. Ten to fifteen percent is not unusual in some areas; as much as twenty percent would be rare.

For brands not mentioned or implied in the above discussion, it's usually a safe bet to figure a discount of fifteen to twenty-five percent from the prices in this *Supplement*, with greater discounts possible in selected situations.

There is no "fair" price for a piano except the one the buyer and seller agree on. The dealer is no more obligated to sell you a piano at a deep discount than you are obligated to pay the list price. Many dealers are simply not able to sell at the low end of the range consistently and still stay in business. It's understandable that you would like to pay the lowest price possible, and there's no harm in asking, but remember that piano shopping is not just about chasing the lowest price. Be sure you are getting the instrument that best suits your needs and preferences and that the dealer is committed to providing the proper pre- and post-sale service.

(Note: Remember that the "street" price discounts suggested above should be subtracted from the "standard" list prices in this *Supplement*, not from the manufacturer's suggested retail price.)

For more information on shopping for a new piano and on how to save money, please see pages 60–75 in *The Piano Book* (fourth edition).

Model	Size	Style and Finish	Price*

Albrecht, Charles

Verticals

Model	Size	Style and Finish	Price*
4300	43"	Contemporary Polished Ebony	3,860.
4300	43"	Contemporary Polished Mahogany	3,960.
4300	43"	Contemporary Walnut	3,660.
4300	43"	Contemporary Polished Walnut	3,960.
4300	43"	Contemporary Cherry	3,660.
4300	43"	Contemporary Polished Ivory	3,960.
4300	43"	Contemporary Polished White	3,960.
4401	44"	Designer Cherry	4,260.
4401	44"	Designer Mahogany	4,260.
4403	44"	Designer Cherry	4,260.
4403	44"	Designer Brown Oak	4,260.
4406	44"	Designer Brown Oak	4,160.
4507	45"	Institutional Polished Ebony	4,060.
4507	45"	Institutional Polished Mahogany	4,160.
4507	45"	Institutional Polished Walnut	4,160.
4507	45"	Institutional Cherry	3,860.
4507	45"	Institutional Walnut	3,860.
4507	45"	Institutional Polished Ivory	4,160.
4507	45"	Institutional Polished White	4,160.
4701	47"	Designer Cherry	4,860.
4701	47"	Designer Mahogany	4,860.
4703	47"	Designer Cherry	4,860.
4703	47"	Designer Mahogany	4,860.
4706	47"	Designer Brown Oak	4,660.
4803	48"	Institutional Polished Ebony	4,860.
4803	48"	Institutional Polished Mahogany	5,260.
4907	49"	Institutional Polished Ebony	5,220.
4907	49"	Institutional Polished Mahogany	5,220.
4907	49"	Institutional Polished Walnut	5,220.
5207	52"	Institutional Ebony or Polished Ebony	6,260.
5207	52"	Institutional Polished Mahogany	6,460.
5207	52"	Institutional Polished Walnut	6,460.
5207	52"	Institutional Polished Ivory	6,260.

Model	Size	Style and Finish	Price*
Grands			
G4701	4' 7"	"Petite" Polished Ebony	8,360.
G4701	4' 7"	"Petite" Polished White	8,760.
G5001	5'	Polished Ebony	8,470.
G5101	5'1"	Polished Ebony	11,260.
G5101	5'1"	Walnut or Polished Walnut	11,760.
G5101	5'1"	Polished Mahogany	11,760.
G5101	5'1"	Polished Ivory	11,260.
G5101	5'1"	Polished White	11,260.
G5209	5' 2-1/2"	Victorian Polished Ebony	10,460.
G5209	5' 2-1/2"	Victorian Polished Mahogany	10,660.
G5209	5' 2-1/2"	Victorian Polished Walnut	10,660.

Astin-Weight

Model	Size	Style and Finish	Price*
Verticals			
375	41"	Santa Fe Oiled Oak	8,740.
375	41"	Spanish Oiled Oak	7,980.
375	41"	Spanish Lacquer Oak	8,180.
375	41"	Italian Oiled Walnut	8,380.
375	41"	Italian Lacquer Walnut	8,580.
375	41"	Regency Oiled Oak	8,380.
375	41"	Regency Lacquer Oak	8,500.
375	41"	Regency Oiled Walnut	8,500.
375	41"	Regency Lacquer Walnut	8,520.
U-500	50"	Oiled Oak	13,380.
U-500	50"	Santa Fe Oiled Oak	14,780.
U-500	50"	Lacquer Oak	13,780.
U-500	50"	Oiled Walnut	13,980.
U-500	50"	Lacquer Walnut	14,380.
Grands			
———	5' 9"	Ebony	35,700.

August Förster — see "Förster, August"

*For explanation of terms and prices, please see pages 28–33.

Model	Size	Style and Finish	Price*

Bachendorff

Verticals

Model	Size	Style and Finish	Price*
RC-115S	44"	Ebony and Polished Ebony	8,760.
RC-115S	44"	Walnut and Polished Walnut	9,160.
RC-115S	44"	Mahogany and Polished Mahogany	9,160.
RC-115S	44"	Cherry and Polished Cherry	9,260.
RC-115S	44"	*Polished Oak*	9,260.
RC-115S	44"	*Polished White*	9,260.
RC-115A	44"	Ebony and Polished Ebony	9,540.
RC-115A	44"	Walnut and Polished Walnut	9,940.
RC-115A	44"	Mahogany and Polished Mahogany	9,940.
RC-115A	44"	Cherry and Polished Cherry	10,040.
RC-115A	44"	*Polished Oak*	10,040.
RC-115A	44"	*Polished White*	10,040.
CF-115	44"	Mediterranean Ebony and Pol. Ebony	7,500.
CF-115	44"	Mediterranean Walnut and Pol. Walnut	7,500.
CF-115	44"	Mediterranean Mahog. and Pol. Mahog.	7,500.
CF-115	44"	Mediterranean Cherry and Pol. Cherry	7,600.
CS-115	44"	Italian Provincial Ebony and Pol. Ebony	7,500.
CS-115	44"	Italian Provin. Walnut and Pol. Walnut	7,900.
CS-115	44"	Italian Provin. Mahog. and Pol. Mahog.	7,900.
CS-115	44"	Italian Provin. Cherry and Pol. Cherry	8,000.
CR-115	44"	Queen Anne Ebony and Polished Ebony	7,500.
CR-115	44"	Queen Anne Walnut and Pol. Walnut	7,900.
CR-115	44"	Queen Anne Mahog. and Pol. Mahog.	7,900.
CR-115	44"	Queen Anne Cherry and Pol. Cherry	8,000.
115SE	44"	Ebony and Polished Ebony	6,480.
115SE	44"	Walnut and Polished Walnut	6,880.
115SE	44"	Mahogany and Polished Mahogany	6,880.
115SE	44"	Cherry and Polished Cherry	6,980.
115AE	44"	Ebony and Polished Ebony	7,140.
115AE	44"	Walnut and Polished Walnut	7,500.
115AE	44"	Mahogany and Polished Mahogany	7,500.
115AE	44"	Cherry and Polished Cherry	7,600.
RC-122S	48"	Ebony and Polished Ebony	9,920.
RC-122S	48"	Walnut and Polished Walnut	10,320.

Model	Size	Style and Finish	Price*
RC-122S	48"	Mahogany and Polished Mahogany	10,320.
RC-122S	48"	Cherry and Polished Cherry	10,420.
RC-122S	48"	*Polished Oak*	10,420.
RC-122S	48"	*Polished White*	10,420.
RC-122A	48"	Ebony and Polished Ebony	9,920.
RC-122A	48"	Walnut and Polished Walnut	9,920.
RC-122A	48"	Mahogany and Polished Mahogany	9,920.
RC-122A	48"	Cherry and Polished Cherry	10,420.
RC-122A	48"	*Polished Oak*	10,420.
RC-122A	48"	*Polished White*	10,420.
RC-128S	50"	Ebony and Polished Ebony	10,700.
RC-128S	50"	Walnut and Polished Walnut	11,100.
RC-128S	50"	Mahogany and Polished Mahogany	11,100.
RC-128S	50"	Cherry and Polished Cherry	11,200.
RC-128S	50"	*Polished Oak*	11,200.
RC-128S	50"	*Polished White*	11,200.
Grands			
RC-160	5' 4"	Ebony and Polished Ebony	25,940.
RC-160	5' 4"	Walnut and Polished Walnut	27,140.
RC-160	5' 4"	Mahogany and Polished Mahogany	27,140.
RC-160	5' 4"	Cherry and Polished Cherry	27,340.
RC-180	6'	Ebony and Polished Ebony	29,940.
RC-180	6'	Walnut and Polished Walnut	31,540.
RC-180	6'	Mahogany and Polished Mahogany	31,540.
RC-180	6'	Cherry and Polished Cherry	31,740.
RC-215	7'	Ebony and Polished Ebony	36,400.
RC-215	7'	Walnut and Polished Walnut	37,200.
RC-215	7'	Mahogany and Polished Mahogany	37,200.
RC-215	7'	Cherry and Polished Cherry	38,400.

Baldwin

Verticals			
660	43-1/2"	Georgian Mahogany	4,820.
662	43-1/2"	Queen Anne Regency Cherry	4,820.
665	43-1/2"	Transitional Country Oak	4,820.
667	43-1/2"	Country French Oak	4,820.

*For explanation of terms and prices, please see pages 28–33.

Model	Size	Style and Finish	Price*
Baldwin (continued)			
2090	43-1/2"	Hepplewhite Vintage Mahogany	5,640.
2095	43-1/2"	Regal Oak	5,640.
2096	43-1/2"	Queen Anne Royal Cherry	5,640.
E101	44"	Continental Polished Ebony	5,880.
243HPA	45"	Ebony	5,940.
243HPA	45"	Golden Oak	5,720.
243HPA	45"	American Walnut	5,940.
5050A	45"	Limited Edition Mahogany	7,820.
5052A	45"	Limited Edition Queen Anne Cherry	7,820.
5057B	45"	Limited Edition Georgian Oak	7,820.
248A	48"	Polished Ebony	8,520.
248A	48"	American Walnut	8,520.
6000	52"	Ebony	11,020.
6000	52"	Mahogany	11,280.
Grands			
M1	5' 2"	Ebony	26,860.
M1	5' 2"	Polished Ebony	27,920.
M1	5' 2"	Mahogany	27,820.
M1	5' 2"	Polished Mahogany	30,220.
M1	5' 2"	Walnut	28,560.
M1	5' 2"	Polished Cherry	29,580.
225E	5' 2"	French Provincial Cherry	33,760.
R1	5' 8"	Ebony	30,220.
R1	5' 8"	Polished Ebony	31,460.
R1	5' 8"	Mahogany	31,520.
R1	5' 8"	Polished Mahogany	33,600.
R1	5' 8"	Walnut	33,380.
R1	5' 8"	Polished Cherry	33,520.
226E	5' 8"	French Provincial Cherry	37,240.
226E	5' 8"	French Provincial Polished Cherry	38,520.
227E	5' 8"	Louis XVI Mahogany	37,240.
L1	6' 3"	Ebony	34,120.
L1	6' 3"	Polished Ebony	35,400.
L1	6' 3"	Mahogany	35,520.
L1	6' 3"	Polished Mahogany	37,660.

Model	Size	Style and Finish	Price*
L1	6' 3"	Walnut	36,600.
L1	6' 3"	Polished Cherry	37,800.
SF10E	7'	Ebony	47,980.
SF10E	7'	Polished Ebony	49,540.
SF10E	7'	Mahogany	49,540.
SD10	9'	Ebony	76,720.
SD10	9'	Polished Ebony	82,100.

ConcertMaster (approximate, including installation by factory or dealer)

Verticals	Playback only / with Perf. Option	8,524./9,736.
Grands	Playback only / with Perf. Option	9,200./10,500.
	With stop rail, add $400	

Note: Discounts may apply, especially as an incentive to purchase the piano.

Bechstein, C.

Verticals

Model	Size	Style and Finish	Price
Balance 116	45-1/2"	Ebony	18,920.
Balance 116	45-1/2"	Polished Ebony	19,340.
Advance 118	46-1/2"	Ebony	21,840.
Advance 118	46-1/2"	Polished Ebony	22,440.
Classic 118	47"	Ebony	17,980.
Classic 118	47"	Polished Ebony	18,960.
Classic 118	47"	Walnut	18,440.
Classic 118	47"	Mahogany	18,440.
Classic 118	47"	Cherry	18,960.
Classic 118	47"	Oak	18,440.
Classic 118	47"	Beech	17,980.
Classic 118	47"	Polished Woods (above)	20,000.
Classic 118	47"	Polished White	20,000.
Contour 118	47"	Polished Ebony	19,840.
Contour 118	47"	Walnut	19,440.
Contour 118	47"	Mahogany	19,440.
Contour 118	47"	Cherry	19,840.
Contour 118	47"	Oak	19,440.
Contour 118	47"	Alder	18,660.
Contour 118	47"	Polished Woods (above)	20,880.
Contour 118	47"	Polished White	20,880.

*For explanation of terms and prices, please see pages 28–33.

Model	Size	Style and Finish	Price*

Bechstein, C. (continued)

Model	Size	Style and Finish	Price*
Classic 124	49"	Polished Ebony	24,000.
Classic 124	49"	Walnut	23,600.
Classic 124	49"	Mahogany	23,600.
Classic 124	49"	Cherry	24,000.
Classic 124	49"	Oak	23,600.
Classic 124	49"	Polished Woods (above)	24,860.
Classic 124	49"	Polished White	24,860.
Elegance 124	49"	Polished Ebony	25,060.
Elegance 124	49"	Walnut	25,060.
Elegance 124	49"	Mahogany	25,060.
Elegance 124	49"	Cherry	25,060.
Elegance 124	49"	Oak	25,060.
Elegance 124	49"	Polished Woods (above)	26,120.
Elegance 124	49"	Polished White	26,120.
Ars Nova 124	49"	Ebony	26,320.
Ars Nova 124	49"	Polished Ebony	26,940.
Concert 11	50"	Polished Ebony	31,660.
Concert 11	50"	Walnut	30,920.
Concert 11	50"	Mahogany	30,920.
Concert 11	50"	Cherry	30,920.
Concert 11	50"	Polished Woods (above)	32,300.
Concert 11	50"	Polished White	32,300.
Concert 8	52"	Polished Ebony	34,880.
Concert 8	52"	Walnut	34,040.
Concert 8	52"	Mahogany	34,040.
Concert 8	52"	Cherry	34,040.
Concert 8	52"	Polished Woods (above)	35,640.
Concert 8	52"	Polished White	35,640.
Concert 8	52"	*Add for sostenuto*	2,960.

Grands

Model	Size	Style and Finish	Price*
K-158	5' 2"	Polished Ebony	58,480.
K-158	5' 2"	Mahogany	56,400.
K-158	5' 2"	Oak	56,400.
K-158	5' 2"	Walnut	58,480.
K-158	5' 2"	Cherry	58,480.

Model	Size	Style and Finish	Price*
K-158	5' 2"	Polished Woods (above)	59,740.
K-158	5' 2"	Polished White	59,740.
K-158	5' 2"	Yew	59,740.
K-158	5' 2"	Classic Polished Ebony	66,840.
K-158	5' 2"	Classic Mahogany	64,760.
K-158	5' 2"	Classic Oak	64,760.
K-158	5' 2"	Classic Walnut	66,840.
K-158	5' 2"	Classic Cherry	66,840.
K-158	5' 2"	Classic Polished Woods (above)	68,100.
K-158	5' 2"	Classic Polished White	68,100.
K-158	5' 2"	Classic Yew	68,100.
M-180	5' 11"	Polished Ebony	63,920.
M-180	5' 11"	Mahogany	61,820.
M-180	5' 11"	Oak	61,820.
M-180	5' 11"	Walnut	63,920.
M-180	5' 11"	Cherry	63,920.
M-180	5' 11"	Polished Woods (above)	66,000.
M-180	5' 11"	Polished White	66,000.
M-180	5' 11"	Yew	66,000.
M-180	5' 11"	Polished Pyramid Mahogany	73,740.
M-180	5' 11"	Polished Mahogany with Inlays	76,860.
M-180	5' 11"	Classic or Chippendale Polished Ebony	72,250.
M-180	5' 11"	Classic or Chippendale Mahogany	70,080.
M-180	5' 11"	Classic or Chippendale Oak	70,080.
M-180	5' 11"	Classic or Chippendale Walnut	72,250.
M-180	5' 11"	Classic or Chippendale Cherry	72,250.
M-180	5' 11"	Classic or Chipp. Pol. Woods (above)	74,340.
M-180	5' 11"	Classic or Chippendale Polished White	74,340.
M-180	5' 11"	Classic or Chippendale Yew	74,340.
M-180	5' 11"	Classic or Chipp. Pol. Burled Walnut	82,180.
M-180	5' 11"	Classic or Chippendale Pol. Varvona	82,180.
A-189	6' 2"	"Academy" Ebony	48,780.
A-189	6' 2"	"Academy" Mahogany	48,780.
A-189	6' 2"	Polished Ebony	57,440.
A-189	6' 2"	Oak	54,300.
A-189	6' 2"	Walnut	54,300.
A-189	6' 2"	Polished Walnut	58,280.

*For explanation of terms and prices, please see pages 28–33.

Model	Size	Style and Finish	Price*

Bechstein, C. (continued)

Model	Size	Style and Finish	Price*
A-189	6' 2"	Cherry	54,300.
A-189	6' 2"	Polished Mahogany	58,280.
A-189	6' 2"	Polished White	58,280.
A-189	6' 2"	Polished Pyramid Mahogany	68,300.
A-189	6' 2"	Polished Mahogany with Inlays	69,560.
A-189	6' 2"	Classic Polished Ebony	66,000.
A-189	6' 2"	Classic Oak	62,660.
A-189	6' 2"	Classic Walnut	62,660.
A-189	6' 2"	Classic Polished Walnut	67,040.
A-189	6' 2"	Classic Cherry	62,660.
A-189	6' 2"	Classic Polished Mahogany	67,040.
A-189	6' 2"	Classic Polished White	67,040.
A-189	6' 2"	Classic Polished Burled Walnut	76,240.
A-189	6' 2"	Classic Polished Varvona	76,240.
B-208	6' 10"	"Academy" Ebony	70,680.
B-208	6' 10"	"Academy" Mahogany	74,860.
B-208	6' 10"	Polished Ebony	80,100.
B-208	6' 10"	Mahogany	80,100.
B-208	6' 10"	Oak	80,100.
B-208	6' 10"	Walnut	80,100.
B-208	6' 10"	Cherry	80,100.
B-208	6' 10"	Polished Woods (above)	83,220.
B-208	6' 10"	Classic Polished Ebony	89,600.
B-208	6' 10"	Classic Mahogany	89,600.
B-208	6' 10"	Classic Oak	89,600.
B-208	6' 10"	Classic Walnut	89,600.
B-208	6' 10"	Classic Cherry	89,600.
B-208	6' 10"	Classic Polished Woods (above)	91,700.
C-232	7' 6"	Polished Ebony	94,620.
C-232	7' 6"	Classic Polished Ebony	103,940.
D-280	9' 2"	Polished Ebony	128,160.

Model	Size	Style and Finish	Price*

Becker, J.

Verticals

Model	Size	Style and Finish	Price
B-120	46"	Continental Polished Ebony	2,070.
B-120	46"	Continental Polished Mahogany	2,070.
B-120	46"	Continental Polished Oak	2,070.
A-121	47"	"Aurora" Polshed Ebony	2,890.
A-121	47"	"Aurora" Polished Mahogany	2,890.
A-121	47"	"Aurora" Polished Oak	2,890.
A-121	47"	"Aurora" Polished Walnut	2,890.
A-122	47"	"Aurora" Chippendale Polished Ebony	2,990.
A-122	47"	"Aurora" Chippendale Pol. Mahogony	2,990.
A-122	47"	"Aurora" Chippendale Polished Oak	2,990.
A-122	47"	"Aurora" Chippendale Polished Walnut	2,990.
A-122	47"	"Aurora" Chippendale Polished White	3,100.

Grands

Model	Size	Style and Finish	Price
GP-155M	5' 2"	"Mignon" Polished Ebony	8,380.

Bentley

Prices are FOB England and do not include duty, freight, and other costs of importing. Oak, ash, and cherry are available at the same price as mahogany. Polished white is available at the same price as polished ebony.

Verticals

Model	Size	Style and Finish	Price
Concord	43"	Polished Ebony	7,455.
Concord	43"	Mahogany	6,165.
Concord	43"	Polished Mahogany	7,455.
Concord	43"	Walnut	6,165.
Concord	43"	Polished Walnut	7,455.
Concord	43"	Teak	6,165.
Concord	43"	Chippendale Mahogany	6,525.
Concord	43"	Chippendale Polished Mahogany	8,025.
Concord	43"	Chippendale Walnut	6,525.
Concord	43"	Chippendale Polished Walnut	8,025.
Heritage	43"	Mahogany	6,750.
Heritage	43"	Polished Mahogany	7,860.
Wessex	46"	Polished Ebony	7,950.

*For explanation of terms and prices, please see pages 28–33.

Model	Size	Style and Finish	Price*

Bentley (continued)

Model	Size	Style and Finish	Price*
Wessex	46"	Mahogany	6,750.
Wessex	46"	Polished Mahogany	7,950.
Wessex	46"	Walnut	6,750.
Wessex	46"	Polished Walnut	7,950.
Berkeley	46"	Mahogany	7,485.
Berkeley	46"	Polished Mahogany	8,730.
Exeter	47"	Polished Ebony	8,760.
Exeter	47"	Mahogany	7,590.
Exeter	47"	Polished Mahogany	8,760.
Exeter	47"	Walnut	7,590.
Exeter	47"	Polished Walnut	8,760.
Berlin	47"	Polished Ebony	8,925.
Berlin	47"	Mahogany	7,935.
Berlin	47"	Polished Mahogany	8,925.
Berlin	47"	Walnut	7,935.
Berlin	47"	Polished Walnut	8,925.
London	47"	Mahogany	8,355.
London	47"	Polished Mahogany	9,405.
Belgrave	47"	Mahogany	8,355.
Belgrave	47"	Polished Mahogany	9,405.
Chelsea	47"	Mahogany	8,355.
Chelsea	47"	Polished Mahogany	9,405.
Salisbury	47"	Mahogany	8,400.
Salisbury	47"	Polished Mahogany	9,450.
Salisbury	47"	Walnut	8,400.
Salisbury	47"	Polished Walnut	9,450.
Esher	47"	Mahogany	8,700.
Esher	47"	Polished Mahogany	9,825.
Esher	47"	Walnut	8,700.
Esher	47"	Polished Walnut	9,825.

Bergmann

Verticals

Model	Size	Style and Finish	Price*
BE-109	43"	Continental Polished Ebony	2,840.

Model	Size	Style and Finish	Price*
BE-109	43"	Continental Polished Red Mahogany	2,930.
BE-109	43"	Continental Polished Brown Mahogany	2,930.
BE-109	43"	Continental Polished Ivory	2,840.
BAF-108	43"	Mahogany	3,350.
BAF-108	43"	Queen Anne Oak	3,350.
BAF-108	43"	Mediterranean Oak	3,350.
BAF-108	43"	Queen Anne Cherry	3,350.
BAF-108	43"	French Provincial Cherry	3,350.
BAF-110	43-1/2"	Mahogany	3,770.
BAF-110	43-1/2"	Queen Anne Oak	3,770.
BAF-110	43-1/2"	French Provincial Cherry	3,770.
BAF-110	43-1/2"	Queen Anne Cherry	3,770.
BE-118	47"	Polished Ebony	3,350.
BE-118	47"	Polished Red Mahogany	3,470.
BAF-118	47"	Cherry	3,580.
BE-121	48"	Polished Ebony	3,560.
BE-121	48"	Polished Red Mahogany	3,680.
BE-131	52"	Polished Ebony	3,770.
BE-131	52"	Polished Red Mahogany	3,890.
Grands			
BTG-150	4' 11"	Polished Ebony	8,810.
BTG-150	4' 11"	Polished Red Mahogany	8,810.
BTG-150	4' 11"	Polished Ivory	8,810.
BTG-157	5' 2"	Polished Ebony	9,860.
BTG-157	5' 2"	Polished Red Mahogany	9,860.
BTG-157	5' 2"	Polished Ivory	9,860.
BTG-175	5' 9"	Polished Ebony	11,120.
BTG-185	6' 1"	Polished Ebony	11,960.

Blüthner

Prices do not include bench.

Verticals

I	45"	Ebony or Polished Ebony	20,480.
I	45"	Walnut or Polished Walnut	21,558.
I	45"	Mahogany or Polished Mahogany	21,446.
I	45"	Cherry or Polished Cherry	21,446.

*For explanation of terms and prices, please see pages 28–33.

Model	Size	Style and Finish	Price*

Blüthner (continued)

Model	Size	Style and Finish	Price*
I	45"	White or Polished White	21,400.
C	46"	Ebony or Polished Ebony	20,620.
C	46"	Walnut or Polished Walnut	21,812.
C	46"	Mahogany or Polished Mahogany	21,602.
C	46"	Cherry or Polished Cherry	21,706.
C	46"	White or Polished White	21,652.
C	46"	Polished Bubinga, Yew, Macassar Eby.	22,850.
C	46"	Saxony Polished Pyramid Mahogany	27,598.
C	46"	Saxony Polished Burl Walnut Inlay	27,864.
A	49"	Ebony or Polished Ebony	26,264.
A	49"	Walnut or Polished Walnut	27,780.
A	49"	Mahogany or Polished Mahogany	27,514.
A	49"	Cherry or Polished Cherry	27,648.
A	49"	White or Polished White	27,576.
A	49"	Polished Bubinga, Yew, Macassar Eby.	29,102.
A	49"	Saxony Polished Pyramid Mahogany	35,150.
A	49"	Saxony Polished Burl Walnut Inlay	35,490.
B	52"	Ebony or Polished Ebony	29,986.
B	52"	Walnut or Polished Walnut	31,718.
B	52"	Mahogany or Polished Mahogany	31,414.
B	52"	Cherry or Polished Cherry	31,564.
B	52"	White or Polished White	31,484.
B	52"	Polished Bubinga, Yew, Macassar Eby.	33,228.
B	52"	Saxony Polished Pyramid Mahogany	40,132.
B	52"	Saxony Polished Burl Walnut Inlay	40,520.

Grands

Model	Size	Style and Finish	Price*
11	5' 1"	Ebony or Polished Ebony	53,174.
11	5' 1"	Walnut or Polished Walnut	56,246.
11	5' 1"	Mahogany or Polished Mahogany	55,648.
11	5' 1"	Cherry or Polished Cherry	55,980.
11	5' 1"	White or Polished White	55,832.
11	5' 1"	Polished Bubinga, Yew, Macassar Eby.	58,924.
11	5' 1"	Saxony Polished Pyramid Mahogany	71,172.
11	5' 1"	Saxony Polished Burl Walnut Inlay	71,856.
11	5' 1"	"President" Polished Ebony	60,222.

Model	Size	Style and Finish	Price*
11	5' 1"	"President" Polished Mahogany	62,630.
11	5' 1"	"President" Polished Walnut	63,234.
11	5' 1"	"President" Polished Bubinga	66,244.
11	5' 1"	Louis XV Ebony or Polished Ebony	62,960.
11	5' 1"	Louis XV Mahogany or Pol. Mahogany	61,528.
11	5' 1"	Louis XV Walnut or Polished Walnut	66,106.
11	5' 1"	"Kaiser Wilhelm II" Polished Ebony	63,506.
11	5' 1"	"Kaiser Wilhelm II" Pol. Mahogany	66,046.
11	5' 1"	"Kaiser Wilhelm II" Polished Walnut	66,682.
11	5' 1"	"Kaiser Wilhelm II" Polished Cherry	66,366.
11	5' 1"	"Ambassador" East Indian Rosewood	73,908.
11	5' 1"	"Ambassador" Walnut	68,434.
11	5' 1"	"Nicolas II" Walnut with Burl Inlay	73,908.
11	5' 1"	Louis XVI Rococo White with Gold	79,384.
11	5' 1"	"Classic Alexandra" Polished Ebony	61,318.
11	5' 1"	"Classic Alexandra" Pol. Mahogany	63,770.
11	5' 1"	"Classic Alexandra" Polished Walnut	64,384.
10	5' 5"	Ebony or Polished Ebony	61,300.
10	5' 5"	Walnut or Polished Walnut	64,838.
10	5' 5"	Mahogany or Polished Mahogany	64,222.
10	5' 5"	Cherry or Polished Cherry	64,532.
10	5' 5"	White or Polished White	64,362.
10	5' 5"	Polished Bubinga, Yew, Macassar Eby.	67,928.
10	5' 5"	Saxony Polished Pyramid Mahogany	82,044.
10	5' 5"	Saxony Polished Burl Walnut Inlay	82,834.
10	5' 5"	"President" Polished Ebony	69,424.
10	5' 5"	"President" Polished Mahogany	72,200.
10	5' 5"	"President" Polished Walnut	72,894.
10	5' 5"	"President" Polished Bubinga	76,364.
10	5' 5"	"Senator" French Walnut with Leather	75,734.
10	5' 5"	"Senator" Jacaranda Rosewd w/Leather	80,782.
10	5' 5"	Louis XV Ebony or Polished Ebony	72,578.
10	5' 5"	Louis XV Mahogany or Pol. Mahogany	69,058.
10	5' 5"	Louis XV Walnut or Polished Walnut	76,208.
10	5' 5"	"Kaiser Wilhelm II" Polished Ebony	73,210.
10	5' 5"	"Kaiser Wilhelm II" Pol. Mahogany	76,138.
10	5' 5"	"Kaiser Wilhelm II" Polished Walnut	76,870.

*For explanation of terms and prices, please see pages 28–33.

Model	Size	Style and Finish	Price*

Blüthner (continued)

Model	Size	Style and Finish	Price*
10	5' 5"	"Kaiser Wilhelm II" Polished Cherry	76,502.
10	5' 5"	"Ambassador" East Indian Rosewood	85,200.
10	5' 5"	"Ambassador" Walnut	78,890.
10	5' 5"	"Nicolas II" Walnut with Burl Inlay	85,200.
10	5' 5"	Louis XVI Rococo White with Gold	91,512.
10	5' 5"	"Classic Alexandra" Polished Ebony	70,684.
10	5' 5"	"Classic Alexandra" Pol. Mahogany	73,512.
10	5' 5"	"Classic Alexandra" Polished Walnut	74,220.
6	6' 3"	Ebony or Polished Ebony	66,856.
6	6' 3"	Walnut or Polished Walnut	70,718.
6	6' 3"	Mahogany or Polished Mahogany	70,044.
6	6' 3"	Cherry or Polished Cherry	70,384.
6	6' 3"	White or Polished White	70,200.
6	6' 3"	Polished Bubinga, Yew, Macassar Eby.	74,086.
6	6' 3"	Saxony Polished Pyramid Mahogany	89,484.
6	6' 3"	Saxony Polished Burl Walnut Inlay	90,346.
6	6' 3"	"President" Polished Ebony	75,718.
6	6' 3"	"President" Polished Mahogany	78,746.
6	6' 3"	"President" Polished Walnut	79,506.
6	6' 3"	"President" Polished Bubinga	83,290.
6	6' 3"	"Senator" French Walnut with Leather	82,602.
6	6' 3"	"Senator" Jacaranda Rosewd w/Leather	88,108.
6	6' 3"	Louis XV Ebony or Polished Ebony	79,160.
6	6' 3"	Louis XV Mahogany or Pol. Mahogany	83,116.
6	6' 3"	Louis XV Walnut or Polished Walnut	77,872.
6	6' 3"	"Kaiser Wilhelm II" Polished Ebony	79,848.
6	6' 3"	"Kaiser Wilhelm II" Pol. Mahogany	83,044.
6	6' 3"	"Kaiser Wilhelm II" Polished Walnut	83,840.
6	6' 3"	"Kaiser Wilhelm II" Polished Cherry	83,440.
6	6' 3"	"Ambassador" East Indian Rosewood	92,926.
6	6' 3"	"Ambassador" Walnut	86,044.
6	6' 3"	"Nicolas II" Walnut with Burl Inlay	92,926.
6	6' 3"	Louis XVI Rococo White with Gold	99,810.
6	6' 3"	"Classic Alexandra" Polished Ebony	77,094.
6	6' 3"	"Classic Alexandra" Pol. Mahogany	80,950.

Model	Size	Style and Finish	Price*
6	6' 3"	"Classic Alexandra" Polished Walnut	80,178.
4	6' 10"	Ebony or Polished Ebony	79,294.
4	6' 10"	Walnut or Polished Walnut	83,876.
4	6' 10"	Mahogany or Polished Mahogany	83,076.
4	6' 10"	Cherry or Polished Cherry	83,478.
4	6' 10"	White or Polished White	83,260.
4	6' 10"	Polished Bubinga, Yew, Macassar Eby.	87,870.
4	6' 10"	Saxony Polished Pyramid Mahogany	106,134.
4	6' 10"	Saxony Polished Burl Walnut Inlay	107,154.
4	6' 10"	"President" Polished Ebony	89,804.
4	6' 10"	"President" Polished Mahogany	93,398.
4	6' 10"	"President" Polished Walnut	94,296.
4	6' 10"	"President" Polished Bubinga	98,786.
4	6' 10"	"Kaiser Wilhelm II" Polished Ebony	94,704.
4	6' 10"	"Kaiser Wilhelm II" Pol. Mahogany	98,490.
4	6' 10"	"Kaiser Wilhelm II" Polished Walnut	99,438.
4	6' 10"	"Kaiser Wilhelm II" Polished Cherry	98,964.
4	6' 10"	"Ambassador" East Indian Rosewood	110,216.
4	6' 10"	"Ambassador" Walnut	102,052.
4	6' 10"	"Classic Alexandra" Polished Ebony	91,438.
4	6' 10"	"Classic Alexandra" Pol. Mahogany	96,010.
4	6' 10"	"Classic Alexandra" Polished Walnut	95,094.
2	7' 8"	Ebony or Polished Ebony	88,624.
2	7' 8"	Walnut or Polished Walnut	93,744.
2	7' 8"	Mahogany or Polished Mahogany	92,850.
2	7' 8"	Cherry or Polished Cherry	93,298.
2	7' 8"	White or Polished White	93,054.
2	7' 8"	Polished Bubinga, Yew, Macassar Eby.	98,208.
2	7' 8"	Saxony Polished Pyramid Mahogany	118,620.
2	7' 8"	Saxony Polished Burl Walnut Inlay	119,760.
2	7' 8"	"President" Polished Ebony	100,370.
2	7' 8"	"President" Polished Mahogany	104,384.
2	7' 8"	"President" Polished Walnut	105,390.
2	7' 8"	"President" Polished Bubinga	110,408.
2	7' 8"	"Kaiser Wilhelm II" Polished Ebony	105,844.
2	7' 8"	"Kaiser Wilhelm II" Pol. Mahogany	104,384.
2	7' 8"	"Kaiser Wilhelm II" Polished Walnut	105,390.

*For explanation of terms and prices, please see pages 28–33.

Model	Size	Style and Finish	Price*

Blüthner (continued)

Model	Size	Style and Finish	Price*
2	7' 8"	"Kaiser Wilhelm II" Polished Cherry	110,608.
2	7' 8"	"Ambassador" East Indian Rosewood	123,182.
2	7' 8"	"Ambassador" Walnut	114,058.
1	9' 2"	Ebony or Polished Ebony	105,726.
1	9' 2"	Walnut or Polished Walnut	111,834.
1	9' 2"	Mahogany or Polished Mahogany	110,768.
1	9' 2"	Cherry or Polished Cherry	111,302.
1	9' 2"	White or Polished White	111,012.
1	9' 2"	"President" Polished Ebony	119,740.
1	9' 2"	"President" Polished Mahogany	124,530.
1	9' 2"	"President" Polished Walnut	125,726.
1	9' 2"	"President" Polished Bubinga	131,714.
—	—	*Jubilee Edition Plate, any model, add'l*	5,980.

Bösendorfer

Prices do not include bench.

Verticals

Model	Size	Style and Finish	Price*
130CL	52"	Polished Ebony	41,778.
130CL	52"	Open-pore Walnut and Polished Walnut	43,978.
130CL	52"	Open-pore Mahogany and Pol. Mahog.	43,978.
130CL	52"	Satin and Polished Pommelé Mahogany	43,978.
130CL	52"	Satin and Polished Pyramid Mahogany	46,178.
130CL	52"	Bubinga and Polished Bubinga	43,978.
130CL	52"	Amboyna and Polished Amboyna	43,978.
130CL	52"	Satin and Polished Bird's-Eye Maple	46,178.
130CL	52"	Open-pore Rio Rosewood	46,178.
130CL	52"	White and Polished White	43,978.

Grands

Model	Size	Style and Finish	Price*
170CS	5' 8"	"Conservatory" Semi-gloss Ebony	57,178.
170	5' 8"	Polished Ebony	79,178.
170	5' 8"	Open-pore Walnut and Polished Walnut	83,578.
170	5' 8"	Open-pore Mahogany and Pol. Mahog.	83,578.
170	5' 8"	Satin and Polished Pommelé Mahogany	83,578.
170	5' 8"	Satin and Polished Pyramid Mahogany	88,858.

Model	Size	Style and Finish	Price*
170	5' 8"	Bubinga and Polished Bubinga	83,578.
170	5' 8"	Amboyna and Polished Amboyna	88,858.
170	5' 8"	Satin and Polished Bird's-Eye Maple	88,858.
170	5' 8"	Open-pore Rio Rosewood	88,858.
170	5' 8"	White and Polished White	83,578.
170	5' 8"	"Johann Strauss" Polished Ebony	84,678.
170	5' 8"	"Franz Schubert" Polished Ebony	84,678.
170	5' 8"	"Franz Schubert" Polished Cherry	96,778.
170	5' 8"	"Senator," any finish	92,378.
170	5' 8"	"Chopin," any finish	114,378.
185	6' 2"	Polished Ebony	83,578.
200CS	6' 7"	"Conservatory" Semi-gloss Ebony	61,578.
200	6' 7"	Polished Ebony	92,378.
200	6' 7"	Open-pore Walnut and Polished Walnut	100,298.
200	6' 7"	Open-pore Mahogany and Pol. Mahog.	100,298.
200	6' 7"	Satin and Polished Pommelé Mahogany	100,298.
200	6' 7"	Satin and Polished Pyramid Mahogany	105,138.
200	6' 7"	Bubinga and Polished Bubinga	100,298.
200	6' 7"	Amboyna and Polished Amboyna	105,138.
200	6' 7"	Satin and Polished Bird's-Eye Maple	105,138.
200	6' 7"	Open-pore Rio Rosewood	105,138.
200	6' 7"	White and Polished White	100,298.
200	6' 7"	"Johann Strauss" Polished Ebony	97,878.
200	6' 7"	"Franz Schubert" Polished Ebony	97,878.
200	6' 7"	"Franz Schubert" Polished Cherry	109,978.
200	6' 7"	"Senator," any finish	105,578.
200	6' 7"	"Chopin," any finish	127,578.
214CS	7'	"Conservatory" Semi-gloss Ebony	68,178.
214	7'	Polished Ebony	107,778.
214	7'	Open-pore Walnut and Polished Walnut	114,378.
214	7'	Open-pore Mahogany and Pol. Mahog.	114,378.
214	7'	Satin and Polished Pommelé Mahogany	114,378.
214	7'	Satin and Polished Pyramid Mahogany	118,338.
214	7'	Bubinga and Polished Bubinga	114,378.
214	7'	Amboyna and Polished Amboyna	118,338.
214	7'	Satin and Polished Bird's-Eye Maple	118,338.
214	7'	Open-pore Rio Rosewood	118,338.

*For explanation of terms and prices, please see pages 28–33.

Model	Size	Style and Finish	Price*

Bösendorfer (continued)

Model	Size	Style and Finish	Price*
214	7'	White and Polished White	114,378.
214	7'	"Johann Strauss" Polished Ebony	113,278.
214	7'	"Franz Schubert" Polished Ebony	113,278.
214	7'	"Franz Schubert" Polished Cherry	125,378.
214	7'	"Senator," any finish	120,978.
214	7'	"Chopin," any finish	142,978.
225	7' 4"	Polished Ebony	114,378.
225	7' 4"	Open-pore Walnut and Polished Walnut	124,058.
225	7' 4"	Open-pore Mahogany and Pol. Mahog.	124,058.
225	7' 4"	Satin and Polished Pommelé Mahogany	124,058.
225	7' 4"	Satin and Polished Pyramid Mahogany	129,338.
225	7' 4"	Bubinga and Polished Bubinga	124,058.
225	7' 4"	Amboyna and Polished Amboyna	129,338.
225	7' 4"	Satin and Polished Bird's-Eye Maple	129,338.
225	7' 4"	Open-pore Rio Rosewood	129,338.
225	7' 4"	White and Polished White	124,058.
225	7' 4"	"Johann Strauss" Polished Ebony	119,878.
225	7' 4"	"Franz Schubert" Polished Ebony	119,878.
225	7' 4"	"Franz Schubert" Polished Cherry	129,778.
225	7' 4"	"Senator," any finish	125,378.
225	7' 4"	"Chopin," any finish	147,378.
225	7' 4"	"Hollein" Red with 24 Karat Gold	145,178.
275	9'	*Polished Ebony*	145,178.
275	9'	*Open-pore Walnut and Polished Walnut*	155,738.
275	9'	*Open-pore Mahogany and Pol. Mahog.*	155,738.
275	9'	*Satin and Polished Pommelé Mahogany*	155,738.
275	9'	*Satin and Polished Pyramid Mahogany*	161,898.
275	9'	*Bubinga and Polished Bubinga*	155,738.
275	9'	*Amboyna and Polished Amboyna*	161,898.
275	9'	*Satin and Polished Bird's-Eye Maple*	161,898.
275	9'	*Open-pore Rio Rosewood*	161,898.
275	9'	*White and Polished White*	155,738.
275	9'	*"Johann Strauss" Polished Ebony*	153,978.
275	9'	*"Franz Schubert" Polished Ebony*	153,978.
275	9'	*"Franz Schubert" Polished Cherry*	162,778.

Model	Size	Style and Finish	Price*
275	9'	*"Senator," any finish*	158,378.
275	9'	*"Chopin," any finish*	180,378.
280	9' 2"	Polished Ebony	153,978.
280	9' 2"	Open-pore Walnut and Polished Walnut	164,538.
280	9' 2"	Open-pore Mahogany and Pol. Mahog.	164,538.
280	9' 2"	Satin and Polished Pommelé Mahogany	164,538.
280	9' 2"	Satin and Polished Pyramid Mahogany	170,698.
280	9' 2"	Bubinga and Polished Bubinga	164,538.
280	9' 2"	Amboyna and Polished Amboyna	170,698.
280	9' 2"	Satin and Polished Bird's-Eye Maple	170,698.
280	9' 2"	Open-pore Rio Rosewood	170,698.
280	9' 2"	White and Polished White	164,538.
280	9' 2"	"Johann Strauss" Polished Ebony	162,778.
280	9' 2"	"Franz Schubert" Polished Ebony	162,778.
280	9' 2"	"Franz Schubert" Polished Cherry	171,578.
280	9' 2"	"Senator," any finish	167,178.
280	9' 2"	"Chopin," any finish	189,178.
290	9' 6"	Polished Ebony	175,978.
290	9' 6"	Open-pore Walnut and Polished Walnut	186,978.
290	9' 6"	Open-pore Mahogany and Pol. Mahog.	186,978.
290	9' 6"	Satin and Polished Pommelé Mahogany	186,978.
290	9' 6"	Satin and Polished Pyramid Mahogany	193,578.
290	9' 6"	Bubinga and Polished Bubinga	186,978.
290	9' 6"	Amboyna and Polished Amboyna	193,578.
290	9' 6"	Satin and Polished Bird's-Eye Maple	193,578.
290	9' 6"	Open-pore Rio Rosewood	193,578.
290	9' 6"	White and Polished White	186,978.
290	9' 6"	"Johann Strauss" Polished Ebony	182,578.
290	9' 6"	"Franz Schubert" Polished Ebony	182,578.
290	9' 6"	"Franz Schubert" Polished Cherry	193,578.
290	9' 6"	"Senator," any finish	189,178.
290	9' 6"	"Chopin," any finish	213,378.
290	9' 6"	"Hollein" Red with 24 Karat Gold	219,780.
all models		"Chippendale," any finish	on request
all models		"Louis XV," any finish	on request
all models		"Baroque," any finish	on request

*For explanation of terms and prices, please see pages 28–33.

Model	Size	Style and Finish	Price*

Boston

Verticals

Model	Size	Style and Finish	Price*
UP-118C	45"	Continental Polished Ebony	7,960.
UP-118C	45"	Continental Polished Walnut	8,680.
UP-118C	45"	Continental Polished Mahogany	8,680.
UP-118E	46"	Polished Ebony	8,460.
UP-118E	46"	Walnut	9,440.
UP-118E	46"	Polished Walnut	9,640.
UP-118E	46"	Polished Mahogany	9,640.
UP-118E	46"	Polished White	9,440.
UP-118A	46"	Art Deco Aniegre	7,990.
UP-118S	46"	Open-Pore Honey Oak	5,990.
UP-118S	46"	Open-Pore Black Oak	5,990.
UP-118S	46"	Open-Pore Red Oak	5,990.
UP-118S	46"	Mahogany	5,990.
UP-118T	46"	Florentine Mahogany	7,990.
UP-118P	46"	Berkshire Cherry	7,990.
UP-126E	50"	Polished Ebony	10,900.
UP-126E	50"	Polished Mahogany	12,580.
UP-132E	52"	Polished Ebony	11,980.

Grands

Model	Size	Style and Finish	Price*
GP-156	5' 1"	Ebony and Polished Ebony	15,720.
GP-163	5' 4"	Ebony	18,880.
GP-163	5' 4"	Polished Ebony	19,300.
GP-163	5' 4"	Mahogany	20,560.
GP-163	5' 4"	Polished Mahogany	21,040.
GP-163	5' 4"	Walnut	20,760.
GP-163	5' 4"	Polished Walnut	21,280.
GP-163	5' 4"	Polished White	19,840.
GP-163	5' 4"	Polished Ivory	19,840.
GP-178	5' 10"	Ebony	21,780.
GP-178	5' 10"	Polished Ebony	22,240.
GP-178	5' 10"	Mahogany	23,200.
GP-178	5' 10"	Polished Mahogany	23,700.
GP-178	5' 10"	Walnut	23,460.
GP-178	5' 10"	Polished Walnut	24,160.

Model	Size	Style and Finish	Price*
GP-178	5' 10"	Polished White	22,720.
GP-178	5' 10"	Polished Ivory	22,720.
GP-193	6' 4"	Ebony	27,580.
GP-193	6' 4"	Polished Ebony	28,280.
GP-193	6' 4"	Walnut	30,720.
GP-193	6' 4"	Polished Mahogany	30,940.
GP-193	6' 4"	Polished White	29,760.
GP-218	7' 2"	Ebony	35,020.
GP-218	7' 2"	Polished Ebony	35,920.

Brentwood—see "Westbrook / Brentwood"

Broadwood, John, & Sons

Prices are FOB England and do not include duty, freight, and other costs of importing. Oak, ash, and cherry are available at the same price as mahogany. Polished white is available at the same price as polished ebony.

Verticals

St. James	44"	Polished Ebony	8,085.
St. James	44"	Mahogany	6,900.
St. James	44"	Polished Mahogany	8,085.
St. James	44"	Walnut	6,900.
St. James	44"	Polished Walnut	8,085.
Berwick	47"	Polished Ebony	9,465.
Berwick	47"	Mahogany	8,100.
Berwick	47"	Polished Mahogany	9,465.
Berwick	47"	Walnut	8,100.
Berwick	47"	Polished Walnut	9,465.
Imperial	47"	Mahogany	9,420.
Imperial	47"	Polished Mahogany	10,590.
Stratford	50"	Polished Ebony	13,575.
Stratford	50"	Mahogany	12,510.
Stratford	50"	Polished Mahogany	13,575.
Stratford	50"	Walnut	12,510.
Stratford	50"	Polished Walnut	13,575.

Grands

Boudoir	6' 1"	Polished Ebony	41,970.

*For explanation of terms and prices, please see pages 28–33.

Charles R. Walter — see "Walter, Charles R."

Chickering

Grands

Model	Size	Style and Finish	Price
CH162	5' 4"	Ebony and Polished Ebony	14,190.
CH162	5' 4"	Polished White	14,190.
CH162FP	5' 4"	French Provincial Cherry	17,158.
CH162QA	5' 4"	Queen Anne Cherry	17,158.
CH176	5' 9"	Ebony and Polished Ebony	16,390.
CH176	5' 9"	Polished Ivory	16,390.
CH176FP	5' 9"	French Provincial Cherry	19,790.
CH176CD	5' 9"	Chippendale Cherry	19,790.
CH176L	5' 9"	Louis XVI Polished Mahogany	19,790.
CH189	6' 2"	Ebony and Polished Ebony	19,190.
CH189L	6' 2"	Louis XVI Polished Mahogany	23,190.

Conn

Verticals

Model	Size	Style and Finish	Price
C433	43"	French Cherry	2,790.
C434	43"	French Oak	2,790.
C435	43"	Oak	2,790.
C436	43"	Cherry	2,790.

Conover Cable

In general, "wood finishes" means mahogany, walnut, cherry, and brown oak. However, even where not specifically indicated, most models are available by special order in any finish.

Verticals

Model	Size	Style and Finish	Price
CC-142	42"	Continental Ebony and Polished Ebony	2,590.
CC-142	42"	Continental Cherry	2,490.
CC-142	42"	Continental Walnut	2,490.
CC-142	42"	Continental Polished Wood Finishes	2,690.
CC-142	42"	Continental Ivory and Polished Ivory	2,590.
CC-142	42"	Continental White and Polished White	2,590.

Model	Size	Style and Finish	Price*
CC-144F	44"	French Provincial Brown Oak	3,390.
CC-144F	44"	French Provincial Cherry	3,390.
CC-144M	44"	Mediterranean Brown Oak	3,290.
CC-144T	44"	Cherry	3,390.
CC-144T	44"	Mahogany	3,390.
CC-145	45"	Ebony and Polished Ebony	2,790.
CC-145	45"	Cherry	2,690.
CC-145	45"	Walnut	2,690.
CC-145	45"	Polished Wood Finishes	2,890.
CC-145	45"	Ivory and Polished Ivory	2,790.
CC-145	45"	White and Polished White	2,790.
CC-118F	46-1/2"	French Provincial Brown Oak	3,990.
CC-118F	46-1/2"	French Provincial Cherry	3,990.
CC-118M	46-1/2"	Mediterranean Brown Oak	3,790.
CC-118T	46-1/2"	Mahogany	3,990.
CC-118T	46-1/2"	Cherry	3,990.
CC-147S	46-1/2"	Ebony	3,590.
CC-147S	46-1/2"	Wood Finishes	3,690.
CC-147S	46-1/2"	White	3,590.
CC-147S	46-1/2"	Ivory	3,590.
CC-121B	48"	Ebony and Polished Ebony	4,590.
CC-121B	48"	Polished Mahogany	4,790.
CC-121F	48"	French Provincial Polished Ebony	3,990.
CC-121F	48"	French Provincial Polished Mahogany	4,190.
CC-121M	48"	Mediterranean Polished Ebony	3,890.
CC-121M	48"	Mediterranean Polished Mahogany	4,090.
CC-131B	52"	Ebony and Polished Ebony	5,390.
CC-131B	52"	Polished Mahogany	5,590.
Grands			
CC-150C	4' 11-1/2"	Wood Finishes and Pol. Wood Finishes	10,060.
CC-150C	4' 11-1/2"	Polished White	9,560.
CC-150C	4' 11-1/2"	Polished Ivory	9,560.
CC-150CKAF	4' 11-1/2"	French Provincial — All Finishes	11,190.
CC-150CKBF	4' 11-1/2"	French Provincial — All Finishes	12,050.
CCIG-50	5'	Ebony and Polished Ebony	7,790.
CCIG-50	5'	Polished Mahogany	8,190.
CC-155C	5' 1-1/2"	Wood Finishes	11,220.

*For explanation of terms and prices, please see pages 28–33.

Conover Cable (continued)

Model	Size	Style and Finish	Price*
CC-155C	5' 1-1/2"	Polished White	10,700.
CC-155C	5' 1-1/2"	Polished Ivory	10,700.
CC-155CKAF	5' 1-1/2"	French Provincial — All Finishes	11,190.
CC-155CKBF	5' 1-1/2"	French Provincial — All Finishes	12,050.
CCIG-54	5' 3"	Ebony and Polished Ebony	9,190.
CCIG-54	5' 3"	Polished Mahogany	9,590.
CC-172	5' 7"	Ebony and Polished Ebony	11,990.
CC-172	5' 7"	Wood Finishes	12,500.
CC-172	5' 7"	Polished White	11,990.
CC-172	5' 7"	Polished Ivory	11,990.
CC-172L	5' 7"	Empire Ebony and Polished Ebony	13,060.
CC-172L	5' 7"	Empire Wood Finishes	13,580.
CC-172L	5' 7"	Empire Polished White	13,580.
CC-172L	5' 7"	Empire Polished Ivory	13,580.
CC-185	6' 1"	Ebony and Polished Ebony	12,840.
CC-185	6' 1"	Wood Finishes	13,360.
CC-185	6' 1"	Polished White	13,360.
CC-185	6' 1"	Polished Ivory	13,360.
CC-185L	6' 1"	Empire Ebony and Polished Ebony	13,920.
CC-185L	6' 1"	Empire Wood Finishes	14,430.
CC-185L	6' 1"	Empire Polished White	14,430.
CC-185L	6' 1"	Empire Polished Ivory	14,430.
All grands	—	*Rosewood or Bubinga Finish, add'l*	1,000.

Essex

Verticals

Model	Size	Style and Finish	Price*
EUP-107C	42"	Continental Polished Ebony	5,190.
EUP-111E	44"	European Polished Ebony	5,750.
EUP-111E	44"	European Polished Mahogany	5,890.
EUP-111F	44"	French Provincial Cherry	6,270.
EUP-111M	44"	Modern Walnut	5,990.
EUP-111R	44"	English Regency Mahogany	5,830.
EUP-111T	44"	Ash	5,870.
EUP-123E	48"	European Polished Ebony	TBA

Model	Size	Style and Finish	Price*

Grands

Model	Size	Style and Finish	Price*
EGP-160	5' 3"	Ebony	14,060.
EGP-160	5' 3"	Polished Ebony	13,790.
EGP-160	5' 3"	Mahogany	15,180.
EGP-160	5' 3"	Polished Mahogany	14,900.
EGP-160	5' 3"	Walnut	15,580.
EGP-160	5' 3"	Cherry	15,820.
EGP-160	5' 3"	Oak	15,500.
EGP-160	5' 3"	Polished White	13,960.
EGP-160	5' 3"	Polished Ivory	13,960.
EGP-183	6'	Ebony	18,100.
EGP-183	6'	Polished Ebony	17,840.

Estonia

Prices include Jansen adjustable artist bench.

Grands

Model	Size	Style and Finish	Price*
168	5' 6"	Ebony and Polished Ebony	19,600.
168	5' 6"	Mahogany and Polished Mahogany	21,560.
168	5' 6"	*Walnut and Polished Walnut*	21,560.
168	5' 6"	Afr. Bubinga and Polished Afr. Bubinga	21,560.
168	5' 6"	*White and Polished White*	21,560.
190	6' 3"	Ebony and Polished Ebony	23,856.
190	6' 3"	Mahogany and Polished Mahogany	26,240.
190	6' 3"	*Walnut and Polished Walnut*	26,240.
190	6' 3"	Bubinga and Polished Bubinga	26,240.
190	6' 3"	*White and Polished White*	26,240.
190	6' 3"	*Chippendale White*	28,200.
273	9'	Polished Ebony	53,800.

Eterna

Verticals

Model	Size	Style and Finish	Price*
ERC 10	44"	Continental Polished Ebony	3,690.

*For explanation of terms and prices, please see pages 28–33.

Model	Size	Style and Finish	Price*

Everett

Verticals

EV-112	44"	Continental Polished Ebony	2,590.
EV-112	44"	Continental Polished Mahogany	2,690.
EV-113	45"	Polished Ebony	2,790.
EV-113	45"	Polished Mahogany	2,890.
EV-115GC	45"	Chippendale Polished Mahogany	3,090.
EV-121	48"	Polished Ebony	3,190.
EV-121	48"	Polished Mahogany	3,290.

Grands

EV-152	5'	Polished Ebony	7,780.
EV-152	5'	Polished Mahogany	8,280.
EV-152	5'	Polished Walnut	8,280.
EV-152	5'	Polished White	8,280.
EV-165	5' 5"	Polished Ebony	8,780.
EV-165	5' 5"	Polished Mahogany	9,280.
EV-165	5' 5"	Polished Walnut	9,280.
EV-185	6' 1"	Polished Ebony	10,580.
EV-185	6' 1"	Polished Mahogany	11,080.
EV-185	6' 1"	Polished Walnut	11,080.

Fazioli

Fazioli is willing to make custom-designed cases with exotic veneers, marquetry, and other embellishments. Prices on request to Fazioli.

Grands

F156	5' 2"	Ebony and Polished Ebony	73,700.
F156	5' 2"	Walnut	76,600.
F156	5' 2"	Polished Walnut	79,100.
F156	5' 2"	Polished Pyramid Mahogany	81,600.
F156	5' 2"	Cherry	76,600.
F156	5' 2"	Polished Cherry	79,100.
F183	6'	Ebony and Polished Ebony	82,000.
F183	6'	Walnut	85,900.
F183	6'	Polished Walnut	88,200.
F183	6'	Polished Pyramid Mahogany	91,300.

Model	Size	Style and Finish	Price*
F183	6'	Cherry	85,900.
F183	6'	Polished Cherry	88,200.
F212	6' 11"	Ebony and Polished Ebony	92,600.
F212	6' 11"	Walnut	96,600.
F212	6' 11"	Polished Walnut	99,300.
F212	6' 11"	Polished Pyramid Mahogany	102,700.
F212	6' 11"	Cherry	96,600.
F212	6' 11"	Polished Cherry	99,300.
F228	7' 6"	Ebony and Polished Ebony	104,000.
F228	7' 6"	Walnut	108,300.
F228	7' 6"	Polished Walnut	110,800.
F228	7' 6"	Polished Pyramid Mahogany	116,200.
F228	7' 6"	Cherry	108,300.
F228	7' 6"	Polished Cherry	110,800.
F278	9' 2"	Ebony and Polished Ebony	133,600.
F278	9' 2"	Walnut	139,200.
F278	9' 2"	Polished Walnut	143,500.
F278	9' 2"	Polished Pyramid Mahogany	148,400.
F278	9' 2"	Cherry	139,200.
F278	9' 2"	Polished Cherry	143,500.
F308	10' 2"	Ebony and Polished Ebony	174,000.
F308	10' 2"	Walnut	181,600.
F308	10' 2"	Polished Walnut	184,000.
F308	10' 2"	Polished Pyramid Mahogany	189,600.
F308	10' 2"	Cherry	181,600.
F308	10' 2"	Polished Cherry	184,000.
All models		*Fourth Pedal, add'l*	6,200.
All models		*Third and Fourth Pedals (set), add'l*	7,700.
All models		*Magnetic Balanced Action, add'l*	8,500.

Feurich

Prices do not include bench.

Verticals

Model	Size	Style and Finish	Price
F 116	45-1/2"	Polished Ebony	10,994.
F 116	45-1/2"	Oak	10,672.
F 116	45-1/2"	Walnut	10,672.

*For explanation of terms and prices, please see pages 28–33.

Model	Size	Style and Finish	Price*
Feurich (continued)			
F 116	45-1/2"	Beech	10,672.
F 116	45-1/2"	Tola	10,828.
F 117 SL	46-1/2"	Polished Ebony	9,490.
F 118	46-1/2"	Polished Ebony	12,302.
F 118	46-1/2"	Oak	12,073.
F 118	46-1/2"	Walnut	12,073.
F 118	46-1/2"	Polished Walnut	13,382.
F 118	46-1/2"	Polished Mahogany	13,382.
F 118	46-1/2"	Beech	12,073.
F 118	46-1/2"	Euoprean Cherry	12,400.
F 118	46-1/2"	Polished European Cherry	13,709.
F 118	46-1/2"	Plum	12,842.
F 118	46-1/2"	Swiss Pearwood	12,727.
F 118	46-1/2"	Platane	12,509.
F 118	46-1/2"	Appel-birch	12,469.
F 118	46-1/2"	Yew	13,164.
F 118	46-1/2"	Polished White	12,790.
F 123	48-1/2"	Polished Ebony	14,208.
F 123	48-1/2"	Oak	14,104.
F 123	48-1/2"	Walnut	14,104.
F 123	48-1/2"	Polished Walnut	15,401.
F 123	48-1/2"	Polished Mahogany	15,401.
F 123	48-1/2"	Beech	14,104.
F 123	48-1/2"	European Cherry	14,311.
F 123	48-1/2"	Polished European Cherry	15,723.
F 123	48-1/2"	Yew	15,183.
F 123	48-1/2"	Rio Palisander	15,764.
F 123	48-1/2"	Polished White	14,747.
F 123	48-1/2"	*Sostenuto System, add'l*	1,246.
Grands			
F 172	5' 8"	Polished Ebony	36,049.
F 172	5' 8"	Pommelé Mahogany	38,644.
F 172	5' 8"	Chippendale Walnut	40,956.
F 172	5' 8"	Altdeutschem Rim, Polished Ebony	41,135.
F 227	7' 5"	Polished Ebony	55,712.
F 227	7' 5"	Pommelé Mahogany	58,929.
F 227	7' 5"	Altdeutschem Rim, Polished Ebony	61,421.

Model	Size	Style and Finish	Price*

Förster, August

Prices do not include bench. Although prices include estimated duty and shipping, because dealers purchase directly from the manufacturer, actual price at time of sale may vary depending on the value of the Euro, the dealer's location, and the shipping method utilized.

Verticals

Model	Size	Style and Finish	Price
116C	46"	Chippendale Polished Ebony	14,049.
116C	46"	Chippendale Walnut and Pol. Walnut	14,691.
116C	46"	Chippendale Mahog. and Pol. Mahog.	14,105.
116C	46"	Chippendale Polished White	14,351.
116D	46"	Continental Polished Ebony	11,989.
116D	46"	Continental Walnut and Pol. Walnut	12,679.
116D	46"	Continental Mahog.and Pol. Mahog.	12,026.
116D	46"	Continental Polished White	12,301.
116E	46"	Polished Ebony	14,049.
116E	46"	Walnut and Polished Walnut	14,691.
116E	46"	Mahogany and Polished Mahogany	14,105.
116E	46"	Polished White	14,351.
125G	49"	Polished Ebony	15,050.
125G	49"	Walnut and Polished Walnut	15,750.
125G	49"	Mahogany and Polished Mahogany	15,098.
125G	49"	Polished White	15,362.

Grands

Model	Size	Style and Finish	Price
170	5' 8"	Polished Ebony	30,753.
170	5' 8"	Walnut and Polished Walnut	31,802.
170	5' 8"	Mahogany and Polished Mahogany	30,810.
170	5' 8"	Polished White	32,038.
170	5' 8"	"Classic" Polished Ebony	34,079.
170	5' 8"	"Classic" Walnut and Polished Walnut	38,474.
170	5' 8"	"Classic" Mahogany and Pol.Mahogany	34,684.
170	5' 8"	"Classic" Polished White	38,653.
170	5' 8"	*Chippendale, additional*	6,672.
190	6' 4"	Polished Ebony	33,711.
190	6' 4"	Walnut and Polished Walnut	34,807.
190	6' 4"	Mahogany and Polished Mahogany	33,824.
190	6' 4"	Polished White	34,996.

*For explanation of terms and prices, please see pages 28–33.

Model	Size	Style and Finish	Price*

Förster, August (continued)

Model	Size	Style and Finish	Price
190	6' 4"	"Classic" Polished Ebony	37,037.
190	6' 4"	"Classic" Walnut and Polished Walnut	41,479.
190	6' 4"	"Classic" Mahogany and Pol.Mahogany	37,699.
190	6' 4"	"Classic" Polished White	41,611.
190	6' 4"	*Chippendale, additional*	6,672.
215	7' 2"	Polished Ebony	38,445.
275	9' 1"	Polished Ebony	71,605.

George Steck — see "Steck, George"

Grotrian

Prices do not include bench.

Verticals

Caret	44"	Polished Ebony	19,000.
Caret	44"	Polished Walnut	20,000.
Caret	44"	Polished Mahogany	20,000.
Classic	49"	Polished Ebony	23,800.
Classic	49"	Polished Walnut	25,400.
Classic	49"	Polished Mahogany	25,400.
Concertino	52"	Polished Ebony	27,200.

Grands

Chambre	5' 5"	Ebony	44,600.
Chambre	5' 5"	Polished Ebony	49,000.
Chambre	5' 5"	Polished Walnut	53,800.
Cabinet	6' 3"	Ebony	49,400.
Cabinet	6' 3"	Polished Ebony	54,000.
Cabinet	6' 3"	Polished Walnut	58,000.
Concert	7' 4"	Ebony	60,800.
Concert	7' 4"	Polished Ebony	65,000.
Concert Royal	9' 2"	Polished Ebony	75,400.

Model	Size	Style and Finish	Price*

Haessler

Prices do not include bench.

Verticals

Model	Size	Style and Finish	Price*
115 K	45"	Ebony and Polished Ebony	13,780.
115 K	45"	Waxed Alder	13,506.
115 K	45"	Beech	13,506.
115 K	45"	Ash	13,506.
115 K	45"	White and Polished White	14,400.
118 K	47"	Ebony and Polished Ebony	15,414.
118 K	47"	Ebony with Walnut Accent	16,680.
118 K	47"	Mahogany and Polished Mahogany	16,242.
118 K	47"	Walnut and Polished Walnut	16,242.
118 K	47"	Cherry and Polished Cherry	16,704.
118 K	47"	Cherry with Yew Inlay, Satin and Polish	17,622.
118 K	47"	Oak	14,564.
118 K	47"	White and Polished White	16,058.
118 KM	47"	Ebony and Polished Ebony	16,334.
118 KM	47"	White and Polished White	17,024.
118 CH	47"	Mahogany and Polished Mahogany	17,622.
118 CH	47"	Walnut and Polished Walnut	18,014.
124 K	49"	Ebony and Polished Ebony	16,520.
124 K	49"	Ebony with Walnut Accent	17,462.
124 K	49"	Mahogany and Polished Mahogany	17,898.
124 K	49"	Walnut and Polished Walnut	17,898.
124 K	49"	Cherry and Polished Cherry	18,426.
124 K	49"	Cherry with Yew Inlay, Satin and Polish	19,348.
124 K	49"	White and Polished White	17,208.
124 KM	49"	Ebony and Polished Ebony	17,160.
124 KM	49"	White and Polished White	17,160.
132	52"	Ebony and Polished Ebony	23,254.

Grands

Model	Size	Style and Finish	Price*
175	5' 8"	Ebony and Polished Ebony	42,346.
175	5' 8"	Mahogany and Polished Mahogany	45,744.
175	5' 8"	Saxony Polished Pyramid Mahogany	57,180.
175	5' 8"	Walnut and Polished Walnut	46,184.
175	5' 8"	Saxony Polished Burl Walnut	57,180.

*For explanation of terms and prices, please see pages 28–33.

Model	Size	Style and Finish	Price*

Haessler (continued)

Model	Size	Style and Finish	Price*
175	5' 8"	Cherry and Polished Cherry	45,962.
175	5' 8"	Polished Bubinga	48,382.
175	5' 8"	White and Polished White	44,464.
186	6' 1"	Ebony and Polished Ebony	47,710.
186	6' 1"	Mahogany and Polished Mahogany	51,536.
186	6' 1"	Saxony Polished Pyramid Mahogany	64,424.
186	6' 1"	Walnut and Polished Walnut	52,034.
186	6' 1"	Saxony Polished Burl Walnut	65,040.
186	6' 1"	Cherry and Polished Cherry	51,784.
186	6' 1"	Polished Bubinga	54,512.
186	6' 1"	White and Polished White	50,096.

Hallet, Davis & Co.

Verticals

Model	Size	Style and Finish	Price*
H-C43R	43"	Oak (round leg)	3,100.
H-C43R	43"	Mahogany (round leg)	3,100.
H-C43F	43"	French Oak	3,100.
H-C43F	43"	French Mahogany	3,100.
H-111GD	44"	Continental Polished Ebony	2,620.
H-111GD	44"	Continental Polished Mahogany	2,680.
H-111GD	44"	Continental Polished Walnut	2,680.
H-111GD	44"	Continental Polished White	2,680.
H-115GC	45"	Chippendale Polished Ebony	2,880.
H-115GC	45"	Chippendale Polished Mahogany	2,920.
H-115GC	45"	Chippendale Polished Brown Mahogany	2,920.
HS-450	45"	Italian Provincial Walnut	3,340.
HS-450	45"	Italian Provincial Mahogany	3,340.
HS-450	45"	Italian Provincial Cherry	3,340.
HS-451	45"	Walnut (round leg)	3,340.
HS-451	45"	Mahogany (round leg)	3,340.
HS-451	45"	Cherry (round leg)	3,340.
HS-452	45"	French Walnut	3,340.
HS-452	45"	French Mahogany	3,340.
HS-452	45"	French Oak	3,340.

Model	Size	Style and Finish	Price*
HS-452	45"	French Cherry	3,340.
H-115WH	46"	Polished Ebony	2,920.
H-115WH	46"	Polished Mahogany	2,970.
H-115WH	46"	Polished Walnut	2,970.
H-121WH	48"	Polished Ebony	3,140.
H-121WH	48"	Polished Mahogany	3,250.
H-121WH	48"	Polished Walnut	3,250.
H-U131XK	52"	Polished Ebony	4,190.
H-U131XK	52"	Polished Mahogany	4,390.

Grands

Model	Size	Style and Finish	Price*
HDG-450	4' 7"	Polished Ebony	9,000.
HDG-450	4' 7"	Polished Mahogany	9,360.
HDG-450	4' 7"	Polished Brown Oak	9,360.
HG-148SR	4' 11"	Victorian Polished Ebony	9,390.
HG-148SR	4' 11"	Victorian Polished Mahogany	9,390.
HG-148SR	4' 11"	Victorian Polished Walnut	9,390.
H-152DP	5'	Polished Ebony	8,390.
H-152DP	5'	Polished Mahogany	8,790.
H-152DP	5'	Polished Walnut	8,790.
H-152DP	5'	Polished White	8,790.
HDG-480	5' 1"	Polished Ebony	10,350.
HDG-480	5' 1"	Polished Mahogany	10,720.
H-165DP	5' 4"	Polished Ebony	9,100.
H-165DP	5' 4"	Polished Mahogany	9,700.
H-165DP	5' 4"	Polished Walnut	9,700.
H-165DP	5' 4"	Polished White	9,700.
H-185DP	6' 1"	Polished Ebony	10,390.
H-185DP	6' 1"	Polished Mahogany	10,790.

Hoffmann, W.

Verticals

Model	Size	Style and Finish	Price*
H-116 Trend	46"	Polished Ebony	10,340.
H-116 Trend	46"	Oak	10,340.
H-116 Trend	46"	Polished Oak	10,900.
H-116 Trend	46"	Mahogany	10,340.
H-116 Trend	46"	Polished Mahogany	10,900.

*For explanation of terms and prices, please see pages 28–33.

Model	Size	Style and Finish	Price*
Hoffmann, W. (continued)			
H-116 Trend	46"	Walnut	10,340.
H-116 Trend	46"	Polished Walnut	10,900.
H-116 Trend	46"	Cherry	10,340.
H-116 Trend	46"	Polished Cherry	10,900.
H-116 Trend	46"	Alder	10,050.
H-116 Trend	46"	Beech	10,050.
H-116 Trend	46"	Polished White	10,900.
H-116 Trend	46"	Chippendale Polished Mahogany	11,890.
H-116 Trend	46"	Chippendale Polished Walnut	11,890.
H-120 Trend	47"	Polished Ebony	11,550.
H-120 Trend	47"	Mahogany	11,550.
H-120 Trend	47"	Polished Mahogany	12,120.
H-120 Trend	47"	Walnut	11,550.
H-120 Trend	47"	Polished Walnut	12,120.
H-120 Trend	47"	Cherry	11,550.
H-120 Trend	47"	Polished Cherry	12,120.
H-120 Trend	47"	Alder	11,280.
H-120 Trend	47"	Beech	11,280.
H-120 Trend	47"	Polished White	12,120.
H-120 Trend	47"	Polished Blue	12,600.
H-120 Trend	47"	Chippendale Polished Mahogany	13,160.
H-122	48"	Chippendale Polished Mahogany	9,600.
H-123-EX	48"	Polished Ebony	8,720.
H-123-EX	48"	Oak	8,460.
H-123-EX	48"	Mahogany	8,460.
H-123-EX	48"	Polished Mahogany	8,860.
H-123-EX	48"	Walnut	8,460.
H-123-EX	48"	Polished Walnut	8,860.
H-123-EX	48"	Cherry	8,720.
H-123-EX	48"	Polished Pomele	9,400.
H-126-PR	49"	Polished Ebony	9,980.
H-126-PR	49"	Polished Mahogany	10,160.
H-126-PR	49"	Polished Walnut	10,160.
H-126-PR	49"	Cherry	9,980.
H-125 Trend	50"	Polished Ebony	12,740.

Model	Size	Style and Finish	Price*
H-125 Trend	50"	Mahogany	12,740.
H-125 Trend	50"	Polished Mahogany	13,500.
H-125 Trend	50"	Walnut	12,740.
H-125 Trend	50"	Polished Walnut	13,500.
H-125 Trend	50"	Cherry	12,740.
H-125 Trend	50"	Polished Cherry	13,500.
H-125 Trend	50"	Beech	12,370.
H-125 Trend	50"	Polished White	13,500.
H-132-R	52"	Polished Ebony	12,480.

Grands

Model	Size	Style and Finish	Price*
H-156	5' 2"	Polished Ebony	26,840.
H-156	5' 2"	Polished Mahogany	29,240.
H-156	5' 2"	Polished Walnut	29,240.
H-156	5' 2"	Polished White	28,300.
H-156	5' 2"	Chippendale Polished Mahogany	31,640.
H-185	6' 1"	Polished Ebony	32,000.
H-185	6' 1"	Polished Mahogany	34,560.
H-185	6' 1"	Polished Walnut	34,560.
H-185	6' 1"	Polished White	33,600.
BH-190	6' 3"	Polished Ebony	34,460.
BH-190	6' 3"	Polished Mahogany	35,720.

Hofmann & Scholz / Mecklenburg

Verticals

Model	Size	Style and Finish	Price*
2000	48"	Polished Ebony	8,980.

Grands

Model	Size	Style and Finish	Price*
2002g	6' 1"	Polished Ebony	30,980.

Hyundai

Verticals

Model	Size	Style and Finish	Price*
U-800	42"	Continental Polished Ebony	3,998.
U-800	42"	Continental Walnut	3,758.
U-800	42"	Continental Polished Mahogany	4,300.
U-800	42"	Continental Polished White	4,300.
U-800	42"	Continental Polished Ivory	3,998.

*For explanation of terms and prices, please see pages 28–33.

Model	Size	Style and Finish	Price*

Hyundai (continued)

Model	Size	Style and Finish	Price*
U-824F	43"	French Walnut	4,998.
U-824F	43"	French Brown Oak	4,998.
U-824F	43"	French Cherry	4,998.
U-824M	43"	Mediterranean Brown Oak	4,998.
U-824M	43"	Mediterranean Walnut	4,998.
U-824M	43"	Mediterranean Cherry	4,998.
U-842	46"	Chippendale Polished Mahogany	5,598.
U-852	46"	Ebony and Polished Ebony	5,598.
U-852	46"	Brown Oak	5,598.
U-852	46"	Walnut	5,198.
U-832	48"	Ebony and Polished Ebony	5,198.
U-832	48"	Walnut	4,998.
U-832	48"	Polished Walnut	5,398.
U-832	48"	Brown Oak	5,398.
U-832	48"	Polished Mahogany	5,398.
U-837	52"	Ebony	5,598.
U-837	52"	Polished Ebony	5,698.
U-837	52"	Walnut	5,598.
U-837	52"	Polished Walnut	5,798.
U-837	52"	Polished Mahogany	5,798.

Grands

Model	Size	Style and Finish	Price*
G-50A	4' 7"	Ebony	9,898.
G-50A	4' 7"	Polished Ebony	9,998.
G-50A	4' 7"	Walnut and Polished Walnut	10,398.
G-50A	4' 7"	Polished Mahogany	10,398.
G-50A	4' 7"	Brown Oak	10,398.
G-50A	4' 7"	Cherry	10,398.
G-50A	4' 7"	Polished Ivory	10,198.
G-50A	4' 7"	Polished White	10,198.
G-50AF	4' 7"	Queen Anne Polished Walnut	11,900.
G-50AF	4' 7"	Queen Anne Polished Mahogany	11,900.
G-50AF	4' 7"	Queen Anne Brown Oak	11,900.
G-50AF	4' 7"	Queen Anne Cherry	11,900.
G-50AF	4' 7"	Queen Anne Polished White	11,900.
G-80A	5' 1"	Ebony	11,398.

Model	Size	Style and Finish	Price*
G-80A	5' 1"	Polished Ebony	11,498.
G-80A	5' 1"	Walnut and Polished Walnut	11,898.
G-80A	5' 1"	Polished Mahogany	11,898.
G-80A	5' 1"	Brown Oak	11,898.
G-80A	5' 1"	Cherry	11,898.
G-80A	5' 1"	Polished Ivory	11,698.
G-80A	5' 1"	Polished White	11,698.
G-80AF	5' 1"	Queen Anne Polished Mahogany	14,098.
G-80B	5' 1"	Chippendale Polished Mahogany	14,098.
G-81	5' 9"	Chippendale Polished Mahogany	15,398.
G-82	5' 9"	Ebony	12,798.
G-82	5' 9"	Polished Ebony	12,898.
G-82	5' 9"	Walnut and Polished Walnut	13,298.
G-82	5' 9"	Polished Mahogany	13,298.
G-82	5' 9"	Polished White	13,098.
G-82AF	5' 9"	Queen Anne Polished Mahogany	15,398.
G-84	6' 1"	Ebony	13,498.
G-84	6' 1"	Polished Ebony	13,598.
G-84	6' 1"	Walnut and Polished Walnut	13,998.
G-84	6' 1"	Polished Mahogany	13,998.
G-85	6' 10"	Ebony and Polished Ebony	17,398.

Irmler

European-made Irmlers have model numbers ending in "E"; Chinese-made Irmlers have model numbers beginning with "P".

Verticals

P110A	43-1/4"	Polished Ebony	3,060.
P110A	43-1/4"	Polished Mahogany	3,120.
P110A	43-1/4"	Polished Walnut	3,120.
M113E	44"	Polished Ebony	7,036.
M113E	44"	Walnut	6,954.
M113E	44"	Polished Walnut	7,300.
M113E	44"	Mahogany	7,300.
M113E	44"	Polished Mahogany	7,126.
M113E	44"	Polished Cherry	7,126.
M113E	44"	Beech	6,954.

*For explanation of terms and prices, please see pages 28–33.

Model	Size	Style and Finish	Price*

Irmler (continued)

Model	Size	Style and Finish	Price*
M113E	44"	Alder	7,300.
M113E	44"	Polished White	7,650.
P120A	48"	Polished Ebony	3,350.
P120A	48"	Polished Mahogany	3,420.
P120A	48"	Polished Walnut	3,420.
M122E	49"	Polished Ebony	7,526.
M122E	49"	Walnut	7,476.
M122E	49"	Polished Walnut	7,650.
M122E	49"	Mahogany	7,824.
M122E	49"	Polished Mahogany	7,650.
M122E	49"	Polished Cherry	7,650.
M122E	49"	Beech	7,300.
M122E	49"	Alder	7,824.
M122E	49"	Polished White	8,170.
P122D	49"	Polished Ebony	3,540.
P122D	49"	Polished Mahogany	3,620.
P122D	49"	Polished Walnut	3,620.
P130	52"	Polished Ebony	4,040.
P130	52"	Polished Mahogany	4,380.
P130	52"	Polished Walnut	4,380.
P130	52"	Polished White	4,320.

Grands

Model	Size	Style and Finish	Price*
F16E	5' 4"	Polished Ebony	23,240.
F16E	5' 4"	Walnut	24,080.
F16E	5' 4"	Polished Walnut	24,640.
F16E	5' 4"	Mahogany	25,200.
F16E	5' 4"	Polished Mahogany	24,080.
F16E	5' 4"	Polished Cherry	24,080.
F16E	5' 4"	Alder	24,640.
F16E	5' 4"	Polished White	24,360.
F18E	5' 11"	Polished Ebony	25,920.
F18E	5' 11"	Walnut	26,760.
F18E	5' 11"	Polished Walnut	27,320.
F18E	5' 11"	Mahogany	27,880.
F18E	5' 11"	Polished Mahogany	26,760.

Model	Size	Style and Finish	Price*
F18E	5' 11"	Polished Cherry	26,200.
F18E	5' 11"	Alder	27,320.
F18E	5' 11"	Polished White	27,040.
F18E	5' 11"	"Classic" Polished Ebony	29,400.
F18E	5' 11"	"Classic" Polished Walnut	30,520.
F18E	5' 11"	"Classic" Mahogany	31,080.
F18E	5' 11"	"Classic" Alder	30,520.
F18E	5' 11"	Chippendale Polished Ebony	29,400.
F18E	5' 11"	Chippendale Polished Walnut	30,800.
F18E	5' 11"	Chippendale Alder	30,800.
F18E	5' 11"	Chippendale Polished White	30,800.

Kawai

Verticals

Model	Size	Style and Finish	Price*
K-18	44-1/2"	Polished Ebony	4,590.
K-18	44-1/2"	Polished Mahogany	5,190.
506S	44-1/2"	Mahogany	3,890.
506S	44-1/2"	Oak	3,890.
606	44-1/2"	Oak	4,490.
606	44-1/2"	French Renaissance Cherry	4,690.
606	44-1/2"	Queen Anne Classic Mahogany	4,790.
606	45"	Queen Anne Cherry	5,990.
606	45"	Spanish Provincial Oak	5,890.
UST-7	46"	Ebony	6,690.
UST-7	46"	Oak	6,690.
UST-7	46"	Walnut	6,690.
UST-8	46"	Ebony	5,590.
UST-8	46"	Walnut	5,590.
UST-8	46"	Oak	5,590.
906	46-1/2"	Country Manor Oak	7,090.
906	46-1/2"	English Regency Mahogany	7,190.
906	46-1/2"	French Provincial Cherry	7,190.
UST-10	48"	Ebony	7,790.
UST-10	48"	Mahogany	7,790.
K-22	48"	Ebony	5,590.

*For explanation of terms and prices, please see pages 28–33.

Model	Size	Style and Finish	Price*
Kawai (continued)			
K-25	48"	Polished Ebony	5,590.
K-25/75	48"	"75th Anniversary" Polished Ebony	5,690.
K-30	48"	Polished Ebony	6,390.
K-30	48"	Mahogany	7,390.
K-30	48"	Polished Mahogany	7,590.
K-30	48"	Polished Snow White	6,790.
K-50	49"	Polished Ebony	7,790.
K-50	49"	Polished Sapeli Mahogany	8,990.
K-50	49"	Walnut	8,590.
K-50	49"	Polished Walnut	8,990.
K-50/75	49"	"75th Anniversary" Polished Ebony	7,990.
K-60	52"	Polished Ebony	10,490.
K-80	52"	Polished Ebony	12,590.
Grands			
GM-10	5'	Ebony	12,290.
GM-10	5'	Polished Ebony	12,390.
GM-10	5'	Polished Mahogany	13,590.
GM-10	5'	Polished Snow White	13,590.
GM-10	5'	French Provincial Polished Mahogany	14,590.
GE-20	5' 1"	Ebony	14,490.
GE-20	5' 1"	Polished Ebony	14,890.
GE-20	5' 1"	Walnut	16,390.
GE-20	5' 1"	Mahogany	16,190.
GE-20	5' 1"	Polished Mahogany	16,590.
GE-20	5' 1"	Polished Sapeli Mahogany	16,590.
GE-20	5' 1"	Polished Snow White	15,990.
GE-20	5' 1"	Polished Ivory	15,990.
GE-20/75	5' 1"	"75th Anniversary" Polished Ebony	15,090.
GE-20F	5' 1"	French Provincial Polished Mahogany	17,990.
GE-30	5' 5"	Polished Ebony	16,590.
RX-1	5' 5"	Ebony	18,590.
RX-1	5' 5"	Polished Ebony	18,990.
RX-1	5' 5"	Walnut	20,370.
RX-1	5' 5"	Polished Walnut	20,990.
RX-1	5' 5"	Polished Sapeli Mahogany	20,590.

Model	Size	Style and Finish	Price*
RX-1	5' 5"	Polished Snow White	19,790.
RX-2	5' 10"	Ebony	21,390.
RX-2	5' 10"	Polished Ebony	21,590.
RX-2	5' 10"	Walnut	23,190.
RX-2	5' 10"	Polished Walnut	24,390.
RX-2	5' 10"	Mahogany and Polished Mahogany	23,190.
RX-2	5' 10"	Polished Sapeli Mahogany	23,390.
RX-2	5' 10"	Oak	22,190.
RX-2	5' 10"	Cherry	23,190.
RX-2	5' 10"	Polished Rosewood	27,590.
RX-2	5' 10"	Polished Snow White	22,590.
RX-2/75	5' 10"	"75th Anniversary" Polished Ebony	21,790.
RX-2F	5' 10"	French Provincial Polished Mahogany	27,390.
RX-3	6' 1"	Ebony	27,390.
RX-3	6' 1"	Polished Ebony	27,990.
RX-3	6' 1"	Walnut	29,990.
RX-3	6' 1"	Polished Sapeli Mahogany	30,590.
RX-3	6' 1"	Polished Snow White	28,990.
RX-5	6' 6"	Ebony	30,990.
RX-5	6' 6"	Polished Ebony	31,190.
RX-5	6' 6"	Walnut	33,990.
RX-5	6' 6"	Polished Sapeli Mahogany	33,990.
RX-5	6' 6"	Polished Snow White	32,590.
RX-6	7'	Ebony	34,790.
RX-6	7'	Polished Ebony	34,990.
RX-7	7' 6"	Ebony	39,790.
RX-7	7' 6"	Polished Ebony	40,190.
RX-7	7' 6"	Polished Rosewood	46,790.
GS-100	9' 1"	Ebony	77,990.
GS-100	9' 1"	Polished Ebony	79,990.
EX	9' 1"	Polished Ebony	109,190.
EX-G	9' 1"	Polished Ebony	115,990.

*For explanation of terms and prices, please see pages 28–33.

Model	Size	Style and Finish	Price*

Kemble

Verticals

Model	Size	Style and Finish	Price*
Oxford	43"	Polished Ebony	7,710.
Oxford	43"	Mahogany	6,990.
Oxford	43"	Georgian Mahogany Lustre	7,710.
Oxford	43"	Polished Mahogany	7,710.
Oxford	43"	Polished Walnut	7,710.
Oxford	43"	Beech	7,710.
Traditional	45"	Polished Ebony with Burr Walnut	8,650.
Traditional	45"	Polished Mahogany	8,350.
Prestige	45"	Cherry with Yew Inlay	9,490.
Empire	45"	Empire Polished Mahogany	9,690.
Windsor	46-1/2"	Polished Ebony with Burr Walnut	8,950.
Windsor	46-1/2"	Georgian Mahogany Lustre	8,750.
Windsor	46-1/2"	Polished Mahogany	8,750.
Windsor	46-1/2"	Empire Polished Mahogany	9,890.
K121Z	48"	Polished Ebony	9,590.
K121Z	48"	Georgian Mahogany Lustre	9,290.
K121Z	48"	Polished Mahogany	9,590.
K121Z	48"	Polished Walnut	9,590.
K131	52"	Polished Ebony	13,350.
K131	52"	Polished Mahogany	13,350.

Kingsburg

Verticals

Model	Size	Style and Finish	Price*
LF-109A	43"	Continental Polished Ebony	4,180.
LF-109A	43"	Continental Polished Mahogany	4,270.
LF-109A	43"	Continental Polished Walnut	4,270.
LF-109A	43"	Continental Polished White	4,270.
LF-109AS	43"	Continental Cherry	4,270.
LF-109AS	43"	Continental Oak	4,270.
LF-109BF	43"	Continental Polished Ebony w/Molding	4,480.
LF-109BF	43"	Continental Pol. Mahogany w/Molding	4,630.
LF-109BF	43"	Continental Polished Walnut w/Molding	4,630.
LF-109B	43"	Polished Ebony (straight leg)	4,480.

Model	Size	Style and Finish	Price*
LF-109B	43"	Polished Mahogany (straight leg)	4,480.
LF-109B	43"	Polished Walnut (straight leg)	4,480.
LF-109B	43"	Polished White (straight leg)	4,480.
LF-109GF	43"	Polished Ebony (curved leg)	4,630.
LF-109GF	43"	Polished Mahogany (curved leg)	4,780.
LF-109GF	43"	Polished Walnut (curved leg)	4,780.
LF-113G	44"	Queen Anne or Mediterranean Walnut	5,340.
LF-113G	44"	Queen Anne or Mediterranean Cherry	5,340.
LF-113G	44"	Queen Anne or Mediterranean Oak	5,340.
LM-115B	45"	Polished Ebony	4,780.
LM-115B	45"	Polished Mahogany	4,780.
LM-115B	45"	Walnut	4,780.
LM-115B	45"	Polished Walnut	4,780.
LM-115B	45"	Oak	4,780.
LM-115B	45"	Cherry	4,780.
LM-115BF	45"	Polished Ebony with Molding	4,990.
LM-115BF	45"	Polished Mahogany with Molding	4,990.
LM-115G	45"	Walnut	4,930.
LM-115G	45"	Cherry	4,930.
LM-115G	45"	Oak	4,930.
LM-116EF	46"	Chippendale Polished Ebony	4,780.
LM-116EF	46"	Chippendale Pol. Mahogany w/Molding	4,990.
LM-116EF	46"	Chippendale Pol. Walnut w/Molding	4,990.
LM-116H	46"	Polished Ebony (straight leg)	4,780.
LM-116H	46"	Polished Mahogany (straight leg)	4,780.
LM-116H	46"	Polished Walnut (straight leg)	4,780.
LM-116H	46"	Pol. Ebony w/Oak or Cherry Accents	4,780.
LM-117C	46"	Walnut	5,980.
LM-117G	46"	Ebony (curved leg)	5,980.
LM-117G	46"	Walnut (curved leg)	5,980.
LT-122B	48"	Polished Ebony (straight leg)	5,530.
LT-122B	48"	Polished Mahogany (straight leg)	5,830.
LT-122B	48"	Polished Walnut (straight leg)	5,830.
LT-122B	48"	Polished White (straight leg)	5,830.
LT-122BF	48"	Pol. Ebony w/Molding (straight leg)	5,980.
LT-122BF	48"	Pol. Mahogany w/Molding (straight leg)	5,980.
LT-122BF	48"	Pol. Walnut w/Molding (straight leg)	5,980.
LT-125GW	49"	Walnut	6,280.

*For explanation of terms and prices, please see pages 28–33.

Kingsburg (continued)

Grands

Model	Size	Style and Finish	Price*
F-150B	4' 11"	Polished Ebony	9,990.
F-150B	4' 11"	Polished Mahogany	10,490.
F-150B	4' 11"	Polished Walnut	10,490.
F-150B	4' 11"	Polished White	10,490.
F-158B	5' 2"	Polished Ebony	14,380.
F-158B	5' 2"	Polished Mahogany	14,980.
F-158B	5' 2"	Polished Walnut	14,980.
F-158B	5' 2"	Polished White	14,980.
F-158B	5' 2"	Polished Ivory	14,980.
F-158BS	5' 2"	Walnut	14,980.
F-158C	5' 2"	Polished Ebony (round leg)	15,580.
F-158C	5' 2"	Polished Mahogany (round leg)	15,580.
F-158C	5' 2"	Polished Walnut (round leg)	15,580.
F-158F	5' 2"	Polished Ebony (French leg)	15,880.
F-158F	5' 2"	Polished Mahogany (French leg)	15,880.
F-158F	5' 2"	Polished Walnut (French leg)	15,880.
F-185B	6' 1"	Polished Ebony	16,480.
F-185B	6' 1"	Polished Mahogany	17,380.
F-185B	6' 1"	Walnut	17,380.
F-185B	6' 1"	Polished Walnut	17,380.
F-185B	6' 1"	Polished White	17,380.
F-185B	6' 1"	Polished Ivory	17,380.
F-185C	6' 1"	Polished Mahogany (round leg)	17,980.
F-185C	6' 1"	Polished Walnut (round leg)	17,980.
F-185F	6' 1"	Polished Ebony (French leg)	17,980.
F-185F	6' 1"	Polished Mahogany (French leg)	17,980.
F-185F	6' 1"	Polished Walnut (French leg)	17,980.

Knight, Alfred

Prices are FOB England and do not include duty, freight, and other costs of importing. Oak, ash, and cherry are available at the same price as mahogany. Polished white is available at the same price as polished ebony.

Model	Size	Style and Finish	Price*
Verticals			
K10 Slimline	44"	Polished Ebony	10,605.
K10 Slimline	44"	Mahogany	8,955.
K10 Slimline	44"	Polished Mahogany	10,605.
K10 Slimline	44"	Walnut	8,955.
K10 Slimline	44"	Polished Walnut	10,605.
K10 Slimline	44"	Teak	8,955.
K10 London	44"	Polished Ebony	11,760.
K10 London	44"	Mahogany	9,885.
K10 London	44"	Polished Mahogany	11,760.
K10 London	44"	Walnut	9,885.
K10 London	44"	Polished Walnut	11,760.
K10 School	44"	Mahogany	9,690.
K10 School	44"	Oak	9,690.
Savoy	48"	Polished Ebony	12,510.
Savoy	48"	Mahogany	11,175.
Savoy	48"	Polished Mahogany	12,510.
Savoy	48"	Walnut	11,175.
Savoy	48"	Polished Walnut	12,510.

Kohler & Campbell

In general, "wood finishes" means mahogany, walnut, cherry, and brown oak. However, even where not specifically indicated, most models are available by special order in any finish.

Model	Size	Style and Finish	Price*
Verticals			
KC-142	42"	Continental Ebony and Polished Ebony	2,590.
KC-142	42"	Continental Cherry	2,490.
KC-142	42"	Continental Walnut	2,490.
KC-142	42"	Continental Polished Wood Finishes	2,690.
KC-142	42"	Continental Ivory and Polished Ivory	2,590.
KC-142	42"	Continental White and Polished White	2,590.
KC-244F	44"	French Provincial Brown Oak	3,390.
KC-244F	44"	French Provincial Cherry	3,390.
KC-244M	44"	Mediterranean Brown Oak	3,290.
KC-244T	44"	Cherry	3,390.

*For explanation of terms and prices, please see pages 28–33.

Model	Size	Style and Finish	Price*

Kohler & Campbell (continued)

Model	Size	Style and Finish	Price*
KC-244T	44"	Mahogany	3,390.
KC-245	45"	Ebony and Polished Ebony	2,790.
KC-245	45"	Cherry	2,690.
KC-245	45"	Walnut	2,690.
KC-245	45"	Polished Wood Finishes	2,890.
KC-245	45"	Ivory and Polished Ivory	2,790.
KC-245	45"	White and Polished White	2,790.
KC-147	46-1/2"	Ebony	3,590.
KC-147	46-1/2"	Wood Finishes	3,690.
KC-147	46-1/2"	Ivory	3,590.
KC-147	46-1/2"	White	3,590.
SKV-465S	46-1/2"	Ebony and Polished Ebony	4,390.
SKV-465S	46-1/2"	Walnut and Polished Walnut	4,590.
SKV-465S	46-1/2"	Mahogany and Polished Mahogany	4,590.
SKV-118FA	46-1/2"	French Provincial Polished Mahogany	5,190.
SKV-118FA	46-1/2"	French Provincial Polished Walnut	5,190.
KMV-47T	46-1/2"	"Millennium" Pol. (Lacquer) Cherry	5,590.
KMV-47T	46-1/2"	"Millennium" Pol. (Lacquer) Mahogany	5,590.
KMV-47F	46-1/2"	"Millennium" French Pol. (Lacquer) Cherry	5,590.
KC-121F	48"	French Provincial Polished Ebony	3,990.
KC-121F	48"	French Provincial Polished Mahogany	4,190.
KC-121M	48"	Polished Ebony	3,890.
KC-121M	48"	Polished Mahogany	4,090.
KMV-48SD	48"	"Millennium" Polished Ebony	5,790.
KMV-48SD	48"	"Millennium" Polished Mahogany	5,990.
KMV-52MD	52"	"Millennium" Polished Ebony	6,390.
KMV-52MD	52"	"Millennium" Polished Mahogany	6,790.

Grands

Model	Size	Style and Finish	Price*
KIG-47	4' 7"	Ebony and Polished Ebony	7,490.
KIG-47	4' 7"	Polished Mahogany	7,890.
SKG-400S	4' 7"	Wood Finishes and Pol. Wood Finishes	9,640.
SKG-400S	4' 7"	Polished Ivory	9,140.
SKG-400S	4' 7"	Polished White	9,140.
SKG-400SKAF	4' 7"	French Provincial—All Finishes (satin)	10,890.
SKG-400SKBF	4' 7"	French Provincial—All Finishes (pol.)	11,290.

Model	Size	Style and Finish	Price*
SKG-500S	5' 1"	Wood Finishes and Pol. Wood Finishes	11,220.
SKG-500S	5' 1"	Polished Ivory	10,700.
SKG-500S	5' 1"	Polished White	10,700.
SKG-500SKAF	5' 1"	French Provincial—All Finishes (satin)	12,410.
SKG-500SKBF	5' 1"	French Provincial—All Finishes (pol.)	12,840.
KIG-52	5' 1-1/2"	Ebony and Polished Ebony	8,790.
KIG-52	5' 1-1/2"	Polished Mahogany	9,190.
SKG-530S	5' 2"	Ebony and Polished Ebony	10,990.
SKG-530S	5' 2"	Dark Mahogany	11,590.
SKG-530SM	5' 2"	Dark Mahogany	12,190.
SKG-530SKBF	5' 2"	French Dark Mahogany	12,990.
SKG-530SKBF	5' 2"	French Cherry	12,990.
SKG-600S	5' 9"	Ebony and Polished Ebony	11,990.
SKG-600S	5' 9"	Wood Finishes and Pol. Wood Finishes	12,500.
SKG-600S	5' 9"	Ivory and Polished Ivory	11,990.
SKG-600S	5' 9"	White and Polished White	11,990.
SKG-600SL	5' 9"	Empire Ebony and Polished Ebony	13,060.
SKG-600SL	5' 9"	Empire Mahogany and Pol. Mahogany	13,580.
SKG-600SL	5' 9"	Empire Ivory and Polished Ivory	13,060.
SKG-600SL	5' 9"	Empire White and Polished White	13,060.
KFM-600S	5' 9"	"Millennium" Ebony and Pol. Ebony	19,100.
KFM-600S	5' 9"	"Millennium" All Other Finishes	20,000.
SKG-650S	6' 1"	Ebony and Polished Ebony	12,840.
SKG-650S	6' 1"	Wood Finishes and Pol. Wood Finishes	13,360.
SKG-650SL	6' 1"	Empire Ebony and Polished Ebony	13,920.
SKG-650SL	6' 1"	Empire Mahogany and Pol. Mahogany	14,430.
KFM-650S	6' 1"	"Millennium" Ebony and Pol. Ebony	21,000.
KFM-650S	6' 1"	"Millennium" All Other Finishes	22,000.
KFM-650SL	6' 1"	"Millennium" Empire Satin/Pol. Ebony	21,900.
KFM-650SL	6' 1"	"Millennium" Empire Pol. Mahogany	22,900.
KFM-700S	6' 8"	"Millennium" Ebony and Pol. Ebony	24,000.
KFM-700S	6' 8"	"Millennium" All Other Finishes	25,000.
KFM-800S	7'	"Millennium" Ebony and Pol. Ebony	25,000.
KFM-850S	7' 4"	"Millennium" Ebony and Pol. Ebony	27,000.
KFM-900S	9' 1"	"Millennium" Ebony and Pol. Ebony	67,990.
All Grands	—	*Rosewood or Bubinga Finish, add'l*	1,000.

*For explanation of terms and prices, please see pages 28–33.

Model	Size	Style and Finish	Price*

Krakauer

Verticals

Model	Size	Style and Finish	Price*
K443	43"	French Cherry	3,190.
K444	43"	French Oak	3,190.
K445	43"	Oak	3,190.
K446	43"	Cherry	3,190.
K110B	43"	Polished Ebony	3,190.
K110R	43"	Polished Mahogany	3,190.
K110T	43"	Polished Walnut	3,190.
K110W	43"	Polished White	3,190.
K120B	48"	Polished Ebony	3,390.
K120R	48"	Polished Mahogany	3,390.
K120T	48"	Polished Walnut	3,390.
K120W	48"	Polished White	3,390.
K122	48-3/4"	*Polished Ebony*	3,500.
K122	48-3/4"	*Polished Mahogany*	3,500.
K122	48-3/4"	*Polished Walnut*	3,500.
K122	48-3/4"	*Polished White*	3,500.
K125	50"	*Polished Ebony*	3,590.
K125	50"	*Polished Mahogany*	3,590.
K125	50"	*Polished Walnut*	3,590.
K125	50"	*Polished White*	3,590.

Mason & Hamlin

Verticals

Model	Size	Style and Finish	Price*
50	50"	Polished Ebony	17,012.

Grands

Model	Size	Style and Finish	Price*
A	5' 8"	Ebony	43,208.
A	5' 8"	Polished Ebony	46,206.
A	5' 8"	Mahogany	46,458.
A	5' 8"	African Mahogany	51,566.
A	5' 8"	Polished Pyramid Mahogany	56,474.
A	5' 8"	Rosewood	51,566.
A	5' 8"	Bubinga	51,566.
A	5' 8"	Polished Bubinga	54,564.

Model	Size	Style and Finish	Price*
A	5' 8"	"Monticello" Polished Ebony	49,220.
A	5' 8"	"Monticello" Mahogany	49,458.
A	5' 8"	"Monticello" Rosewood	59,956.
BB	7'	Ebony	56,498.
BB	7'	Polished Ebony	58,122.
BB	7'	Mahogany	58,498.
BB	7'	African Mahogany	65,484.
BB	7'	Polished Pyramid Mahogany	69,648.
BB	7'	Rosewood	65,484.
BB	7'	Bubinga	65,484.
BB	7'	Polished Bubinga	67,108.
BB	7'	"Monticello" Polished Ebony	60,898.
BB	7'	"Monticello" Mahogany	61,498.
BB	7'	"Monticello" Rosewood	75,472.

Mecklenburg — see "Hofmann & Scholz / Mecklenburg"

Niendorf

Prices do not include bench. Although prices include estimated duty and shipping, because dealers purchase directly from the manufacturer, actual price at time of sale may vary depending on the value of the Euro, the dealer's location, and the shipping method utilized.

Grands

145	4' 9"	Polished Ebony	22,144.
145	4' 9"	Polished Dark Mahogany	22,144.
145	4' 9"	Polished Medium Walnut	22,144.
145	4' 9"	Chippendale Polished Ebony	22,862.
145	4' 9"	Chippendale Polished Dark Mahogany	22,862.
145	4' 9"	Chippendale Polished Medium Walnut	22,862.
182	6'	Polished Ebony	25,641.
182	6'	Polished Dark Mahogany	25,641.
182	6'	Polished Medium Walnut	25,641.

*For explanation of terms and prices, please see pages 28–33.

Model	Size	Style and Finish	Price*

Nordiska

Verticals

Model	Size	Style and Finish	Price*
112-F	44"	Continental Polished Ebony	2,780.
112-F	44"	Continental Polished Walnut	2,780.
112-F	44"	Continental Polished Mahogany	2,780.
114-MC	45"	French Polished Walnut	3,780.
114-MC	45"	French Polished Mahogany	3,780.
114-MCH	45"	Polished Walnut	3,780.
114-MCH	45"	Polished Mahogany	3,780.
116-C	46"	Polished Ebony	3,180.
116-C	46"	Polished Walnut	3,180.
116-C	46"	Polished Mahogany	3,180.
118-CH	47"	Polished Ebony	3,380.
118-CH	47"	Walnut	3,380.
120-C	48"	Polished Ebony	3,780.
120-C	48"	Polished Mahogany	3,780.
120-C	48"	Polished Walnut	3,780.
120-C	48"	Polished Dark Walnut	3,780.
122-C	48"	Polished Ebony	3,780.
122-C	48"	Polished Mahogany	3,780.
126-CA	50"	Polished Ebony	4,980.
126-CA	50"	Walnut	4,980.

Grands

Model	Size	Style and Finish	Price*
152-C	5'	Polished Ebony	7,980.
152-C	5'	Mahogany	8,380.
152-C	5'	Polished Mahogany	8,380.
152-C	5'	Polished Dark Walnut	8,380.
152-DC	5'	Demi-Chippendale Polished Ebony	8,900.
152-DC	5'	Demi-Chippendale Polished Mahogany	9,180.
152-DC	5'	Demi-Chippendale Pol. Dark Walnut	9,180.
165-CM	5' 5"	Polished Ebony	9,180.
165-CM	5' 5"	Mahogany	9,500.
165-CM	5' 5"	Polished Mahogany	9,500.
165-CM	5' 5"	Polished Dark Walnut	9,500.
165-DC	5' 5"	Demi-Chippendale Polished Ebony	10,180.
165-DC	5' 5"	Demi-Chippendale Polished Mahogany	10,500.
165-DC	5' 5"	Demi-Chippendale Pol. Dark Walnut	10,500.

Model	Size	Style and Finish	Price*
165-R	5' 5"	Regency Polished Ebony	9,780.
165-R	5' 5"	Regency Polished Mahogany	10,100.
185-C	6' 1"	Polished Ebony	10,980.
185-C	6' 1"	Polished Dark Walnut	11,300.
185-I	6' 1"	Imperial Polished Ebony	11,580.
185-I	6' 1"	Imperial Polished Mahogany	11,900.

Pearl River

Verticals

UP-108D1	42-1/2"	Continental Polished Ebony	2,670.
UP-108D1	42-1/2"	Continental Polished Mahogany	2,720.
UP-108D1	42-1/2"	Continental Polished Light Walnut	2,720.
UP-108D1	42-1/2"	Continental Polished White	2,770.
UP-108M2	42-1/2"	Chippendale Polished Ebony	2,800.
UP-108M2	42-1/2"	Chippendale Polished Mahogany	2,850.
UP-108M2	42-1/2"	Chippendale Polished Light Walnut	2,850.
UP-108T2	42-1/2"	Euro-Studio Polished Ebony	2,900.
UP-108T2	42-1/2"	Euro-Studio Polished Mahogany	2,950.
UP-108T2	42-1/2"	Euro-Studio Polished Light Walnut	2,950.
UP-108T2	42-1/2"	Euro-Studio Polished White	2,990.
UP-110P1	43"	Walnut (Boston fallboard)	3,360.
UP-110P1	43"	Cherry (Boston fallboard)	3,360.
UP-110P2	43"	Country French Oak	3,460.
UP-110P2	43"	Country French Cherry	3,460.
UP-110P3	43"	"Amerasian" Ebony	3,540.
UP-110P3	43"	"Amerasian" Mahogany	3,590.
UP-110P5	43"	Walnut (Boston fallboard)	3,460.
UP-110P5	43"	Cherry (Boston fallboard)	3,460.
UP-110P6	43"	French Provincial Cherry	3,660.
UP-115M1	45"	Polished Ebony (school)	2,930.
UP-115M1	45"	Polished Walnut (school)	2,930.
UP-115P	45"	Polished American Walnut	3,780.
UP-115P	45"	Cherry	3,780.
UP-118M	47"	Polished Ebony	3,060.
UP-118M	47"	Polished Mahogany	3,110.
UP-118M	47"	Polished Walnut	3,110.

*For explanation of terms and prices, please see pages 28–33.

Pearl River (continued)

Model	Size	Style and Finish	Price*
UP-118M	47"	Polished Light Walnut	3,110.
UP-118M	47"	Polished White	3,150.
UP-125M1	49"	Polished Ebony (with Yamaha)	4,480.
UP-130T2	51"	Euro Special Design Pol. Mahogany	5,020.
Grands			
GP-142	4' 7"	Ebony and Polished Ebony	8,140.
GP-142	4' 7"	Polished Mahogany	8,470.
GP-142	4' 7"	Polished Walnut	8,470.
GP-142	4' 7"	Polished White	8,470.
GP-159	5' 3"	Polished Ebony	9,840.
GP-159	5' 3"	Polished Mahogany	10,170.
GP-159	5' 3"	Polished Walnut	10,170.
GP-159	5' 3"	Polished White	10,170.
GP-183	6'	Polished Ebony	13,730.
GP-183	6'	Polished Mahogany	14,050.
GP-188	6' 4"	Polished Ebony	16,200.
GP-188	6' 4"	Polished Mahogany	16,700.
GP-188	6' 4"	Polished Walnut	16,700.
GP-213	7'	Polished Ebony	17,980.
GP-275	9'	Polished Ebony	on request

Perzina, Gebr.

Model	Size	Style and Finish	Price*
Verticals			
GD-118A	47"	Continental Polished Ebony	5,990.
GD-121B	48"	Polished Ebony	6,880.
GD-121B	48"	Polished Mahogany	7,180.
GD-121B	48"	Polished Walnut	7,180.
GS-128B	51"	Polished Ebony	7,480.
GS-128B	51"	Polished Mahogany	7,990.

Petrof

Note: Prices below do not include bench. Add from $220 to $630 (most are under $400), depending on choice of bench.

Verticals

Model	Size	Style and Finish	Price*
100-B	42"	"Barok" Polished Walnut	7,100.
100-B	42"	"Barok" Polished Flame Mahogany	7,100.
105-V	43"	"Futura" Polished Walnut	5,380.
105-V	43"	"Futura" Polished Mahogany	5,380.
115-I	45"	Demi-Chippendale Polished Ebony	6,700.
115-I	45"	Demi-Chippendale Polished Walnut	6,700.
115-I	45"	Demi-Chippendale Pol. Flame Mahog.	6,700.
115-I	45"	Demi-Chipp. Pol. Walnut w/Designer Panel	6,900.
115-I	45"	Demi-Chipp. Pol. Mahog. w/Designer Panel	6,900.
115-IC	45"	Chippendale Polished Ebony	6,980.
115-IC	45"	Chippendale Polished Walnut	6,980.
115-IC	45"	Chippendale Polished Flame Mahogany	6,980.
115-II	45"	Continental Polished Ebony	5,980.
115-II	45"	Continental Polished Walnut	5,980.
115-II	45"	Continental Polished Flame Mahogany	5,980.
115-II	45"	Continental Polished Oak	5,980.
115-IID	45"	Polished Ebony	6,780.
115-IID	45"	Polished Walnut	6,780.
115-IID	45"	Polished Flame Mahogany	6,780.
115-V	45"	Polished Ebony	6,580.
115-V	45"	Polished Walnut	6,580.
115-V	45"	Polished Flame Mahogany	6,580.
115-VI	45"	Polished Ebony	6,380.
115-VI	45"	Polished Walnut	6,380.
115-VI	45"	Polished Flame Mahogany	6,380.
115-VII	45"	Polished Burl Walnut Veneer	6,580.
125-III	50"	Polished Walnut	7,700.
125-III	50"	Polished Flame Mahogany	7,700.
125-III	50"	Polished Mahogany w/ Designer Panel	7,900.
125-IV	50"	Polished Ebony	7,780.
126	50"	"Elegante" Pol. Ebony w/ Walnut/Gold	8,300.
131	52"	Polished Ebony	10,500.

*For explanation of terms and prices, please see pages 28–33.

Model	Size	Style and Finish	Price*

Petrof (continued)

Model	Size	Style and Finish	Price*
131	52"	Polished Walnut	10,500.
131	52"	Polished Flame Mahogany	10,500.
135	53"	Polished Ebony	14,500.

Grands

Model	Size	Style and Finish	Price*
V	5' 3"	Polished Ebony	19,980.
V	5' 3"	Polished Walnut	19,980.
V	5' 3"	Polished Flame Mahogany	19,980.
V	5' 3"	Demi-Chippendale Polished Ebony	22,400.
V	5' 3"	Demi-Chippendale Polished Walnut	22,400.
V	5' 3"	Demi-Chippendale Pol. Flame Mahog.	22,400.
IV	5' 8"	Polished Ebony	21,600.
IV	5' 8"	Polished Walnut	21,600.
IV	5' 8"	Polished Flame Mahogany	21,600.
IV	5' 8"	Demi-Chippendale Polished Ebony	23,600.
IV	5' 8"	Demi-Chippendale Polished Walnut	23,600.
IV	5' 8"	Demi-Chippendale Pol. Flame Mahog.	23,600.
IV C	5' 8"	Chippendale Polished Ebony	26,600.
IV C	5' 8"	Chippendale Polished Walnut	26,600.
IV C	5' 8"	Chippendale Polished Flame Mahogany	26,600.
III	6' 4"	Polished Ebony	25,800.
III	6' 4"	Polished Walnut	25,800.
III	6' 4"	Polished Flame Mahogany	25,800.
II	7' 9"	"Symphony" Polished Ebony	39,000.
I	9' 3"	"Mondial" Polished Ebony	49,000.
P1	9' 3"	"Mistral" Polished Ebony	68,000.

PianoDisc

Prices for PianoDisc and QuietTime systems vary by piano manufacturer and installer. The following are suggested retail prices from PianoDisc. The usual dealer discounts may apply, especially as an incentive to purchase a piano.

228 CFX System, "factory-installed" or retrofitted:

Playback only	6,489.
Add for SymphonyPro Sound Module	1,429.

Model	Size	Style and Finish	Price*
		Add for TFT MIDI Record system	1,429.
		Add for amplified speakers, pair	824.
		Add for MX (Music Expansion) Basic	1,429.
		Add for MX (Music Expansion) Platinum	1,869.
		Add for PianoAmp	505.
		Add for PianoMute Rail	439.
		Add for Home Theater Master Remote	499.
PianoCD System			5,499.
QuietTime GT System (TFT MIDI Strip, MIDI interface board, pedal switches, cable, headphones, power supply, PianoMute rail)			2,188.
MIDI Controller (TFT MIDI Strip, MIDI interface board, pedal switches, cable, power supply)			2,034.

Pleyel

Verticals

Model	Size	Style and Finish	Price*
PL 118	47"	Polished Ebony	12,520.
PL 118	47"	Polished Ebony with Cherry Decor	13,080.
PL 118	47"	Polished Mahogany	13,920.
PL 118	47"	Walnut with Marquetry	12,800.
PL 124	49"	Polished Ebony	13,920.
PL 124	49"	Polished Ebony with Cherry	14,500.
PL 124	49"	Cherry/Walnut with Marquetry	14,200.
PL 131	51"	Polished Ebony	17,180.
PL 131	51"	Polished Ebony with Sostenuto	19,380.
PL 131	51"	Polished Mahogany	18,780.

Grands

Model	Size	Style and Finish	Price*
PL 170	5' 8"	Polished Ebony	37,800.
PL 170	5' 8"	Polished Mahogany	45,800.
PL 170	5' 8"	Walnut with Marquetry	45,800.
PL 190	6' 3"	Polished Ebony	43,800.
PL 190	6' 3"	Cherry with Marquetry	53,000.
PL 190	6' 3"	Polished Mahogany	53,000.

*For explanation of terms and prices, please see pages 28–33.

Pramberger

Verticals

Model	Size	Style and Finish	Price*
JP-48	48"	Polished Ebony	7,390.
JP-48	48"	Bubinga	7,990.
JP-48	48"	Rosewood	7,990.
JP-48	48"	Cherry	7,990.
JP-52	52"	Polished Ebony	9,390.
JP-52	52"	Bubinga	9,990.
JP-52	52"	Rosewood	9,990.

Grands

Model	Size	Style and Finish	Price*
JP-175	5' 9"	Polished Ebony	17,390.
JP-175	5' 9"	Polished Ebony with Pommele Inlay	18,190.
JP-175	5' 9"	Polished Red Mahogany	18,990.
JP-175	5' 9"	Polished Brown Mahogany	18,990.
JP-175	5' 9"	Polished Kewazinga Bubinga	20,590.
JP-185	6' 1"	Polished Ebony	21,990.
JP-185	6' 1"	Polished Ebony with Pommele Inlay	22,990.
JP-185	6' 1"	Polished Red Mahogany	23,990.
JP-185	6' 1"	Polished Brown Mahogany	23,990.
JP-185	6' 1"	Polished Kewazinga Bubinga	25,990.
JP-185	6' 1"	Polished Santos Rosewood	27,990.
JP-185	6' 1"	Polished African Pommele	28,990.
JP-208	6' 10"	Polished Ebony	25,990.
JP-208	6' 10"	Polished Ebony with Pommele Inlay	27,190.
JP-208	6' 10"	Polished Kewazinga Bubinga	30,990.
JP-208	6' 10"	Polished Santos Rosewood	32,990.
JP-208	6' 10"	Polished African Pommele	34,500.
JP-228	7' 6"	Polished Ebony	34,190.

QRS / Pianomation

Prices for Pianomation systems vary by piano manufacturer, installer, and accessories. The following are approximate retail prices from QRS. The usual dealer discounts may apply, especially as an incentive to purchase a piano.

Model	Size	Style and Finish	Price*
Pianomation:		2000C Player System	5,220.
		2000CD+ Player System, incl. speaker	5,925.
		AMC Player System with CD and	
		floppy drives, speaker	7,075.
		With above and LiteSwitch Record	8,075.
		With above and OptiScan Record	8,575.
Playola:		With 2000C Player System	6,000.
		With 2000CD+ Player System	6,750.
Practice Session:		Lite (LiteSwitch Record, Piano-Only sound,	
		mute rail)	950.
		Opti (OptiScan Record, Piano-Only sound,	
		mute rail)	1,350.

Ridgewood—see "Sagenhaft / Ridgewood"

Ritmüller

Verticals

Model	Size	Style and Finish	Price*
UP-110R2	43-1/2"	"Elegant" Continental Polished Ebony	3,090.
UP-110R2	43-1/2"	"Elegant" Continental Pol. Mahogany	3,140.
UP-110R2	43-1/2"	"Elegant" Continental Polished Walnut	3,140.
UP-110R2	43-1/2"	"Elegant" Continental Polished White	3,140.
UP-118R1	46-1/2"	"Designer" Polished Ebony	3,580.
UP-118R1	46-1/2"	"Designer" Polished Mahogany	3,640.
UP-118R1	46-1/2"	"Designer" Polished Walnut	3,640.
UP-118R2	46-1/2"	"Scandinavian Design" Polished Ebony	3,420.
UP-118R2	46-1/2"	"Scandinavian Design" Pol. Mahogany	3,900.
UP-118R2	46-1/2"	"Scandinavian Design" Pol. Catalpa	3,900.
UP-120R	48"	Polished Ebony	3,920.
UP-120R	48"	Polished Mahogany	3,980.
UP-120R	48"	Polished Walnut	3,980.
UP-120R1	48"	"European Designer" Pol. Ebony w/Mahog.	4,040.
UP-120R1	48"	"European Designer" Pol. Emerald w/Oak	4,090.
UP-120R2	48"	Chippendale Walnut	4,390.
UP-120R2	48"	Chippendale Cherry	4,390.
UP-120R3	48"	"Euro Modern" Polished Ebony	4,380.

*For explanation of terms and prices, please see pages 28–33.

Model	Size	Style and Finish	Price*

Ritmüller (continued)

UP-123R	48"	"Classic Euro" Mahogany	4,940.
UP-123R	48"	"Classic Euro" Polished Mahogany	4,940.
UP-123R	48"	"Classic Euro" Polished Walnut	4,940.
UP-126R	50"	"Designer Upright" Pol. Eb. w/Burl Walnut	5,170.
UP-130R	51"	Ebony	5,400.

Grands

GP-142R	4' 7"	Polished Ebony	8,630.
GP-142R	4' 7"	Polished Mahogany	8,980.
GP-142R	4' 7"	Polished Walnut	8,980.
GP-142R	4' 7"	Polished White	8,980.
GP-142R1	4' 7"	Polished Ebony	8,530.
GP-142R1	4' 7"	Polished Mahogany	8,880.
GP-142R1	4' 7"	Polished Walnut	8,880.
GP-142R1	4' 7"	Polished White	8,880.
GP-159R	5' 3"	Polished Ebony	11,560.
GP-159R	5' 3"	Polished Mahogany	11,880.
GP-159R	5' 3"	Polished Walnut	11,880.
GP-159R	5' 3"	Polished White	11,880.
GP-159R1	5' 3"	"Euro-Modern" Polished Ebony	11,360.
GP-159R1	5' 3"	"Euro-Modern" Polished Mahogany	11,680.
GP-159R1	5' 3"	"Euro-Modern" Polished Walnut	11,680.
GP-183R	6'	Polished Ebony	14,440.
GP-183R	6'	Polished Mahogany	14,760.
GP-183R1	6'	Polished Ebony	14,340.
GP-183R1	6'	Polished Mahogany	14,660.

Sagenhaft / Ridgewood

Verticals

S-112	44-1/2"	Continental Polished Ebony	2,460.
S-112	44-1/2"	Continental Polished Mahogany	2,560.

Grands

SG-152	5'	Polished Ebony	8,490.
SG-152	5'	Polished Mahogany	8,890.
SG-152	5'	Polished Walnut	8,890.
SG-165	5' 5"	Polished Ebony	9,190.

Samick

In general, "wood finishes" means mahogany, walnut, cherry, and brown oak. However, even where not specifically indicated, most models are available by special order in any finish.

Verticals

Model	Size	Style and Finish	Price*
JS-042	42"	Continental Ebony and Polished Ebony	2,590.
JS-042	42"	Continental Cherry	2,490.
JS-042	42"	Continental Walnut	2,490.
JS-042	42"	Continental Polished Wood Finishes	2,690.
JS-042	42"	Continental Polished Ivory	2,590.
JS-042	42"	Continental Polished White	2,590.
JS-143F	44"	French Provincial Brown Oak	3,390.
JS-143F	44"	French Provincial Cherry	3,390.
JS-143M	44"	Mediterranean Brown Oak	3,290.
JS-143T	44"	Cherry	3,390.
JS-143T	44"	Mahogany	3,390.
JS-115	45"	Ebony and Polished Ebony	2,790.
JS-115	45"	Cherry	2,690.
JS-115	45"	Walnut	2,690.
JS-115	45"	Polished Wood Finishes	2,890.
JS-115	45"	Ivory and Polished Ivory	2,790.
JS-115	45"	White and Polished White	2,790.
JS-118F	46-1/2"	French Provincial Brown Oak	3,990.
JS-118F	46-1/2"	French Provincial Cherry	3,990.
JS-118M	46-1/2"	Mediterranean Brown Oak	3,790.
JS-118T	46-1/2"	Mahogany	3,990.
JS-118T	46-1/2"	Cherry	3,990.
JS-147	46-1/2"	Ebony	3,590.
JS-147	46-1/2"	Wood Finishes	3,690.
JS-147	46-1/2"	White	3,590.
JS-147	46-1/2"	Ivory	3,590.
SU-147S	46-1/2"	Ebony	4,390.
SU-147S	46-1/2"	Wood Finishes	4,590.
SU-118FA	46-1/2"	French Provincial Polished Mahogany	5,190.
SU-118FA	46-1/2"	French Provincial Polished Walnut	5,190.
JS-121F	48"	French Provincial Polished Ebony	3,990.

*For explanation of terms and prices, please see pages 28–33.

Model	Size	Style and Finish	Price*

Samick (continued)

Model	Size	Style and Finish	Price*
JS-121F	48"	French Provincial Polished Mahogany	4,190.
JS-121M	48"	Polished Ebony	3,890.
JS-121M	48"	Polished Mahogany	4,090.
SU-121B	48"	Ebony and Polished Ebony	4,590.
SU-121B	48"	Polished Mahogany	4,790.
SU-131B	52"	Ebony and Polished Ebony	5,390.
SU-131B	52"	Polished Mahogany	5,590.

Grands

Model	Size	Style and Finish	Price*
SIG-50	4' 11-1/2"	Ebony and Polished Ebony	7,790.
SIG-50	4' 11-1/2"	Polished Mahogany	8,190.
SG-150C	4' 11-1/2"	Wood Finishes and Pol. Wood Finishes	10,060.
SG-150C	4' 11-1/2"	Polished White	9,560.
SG-150C	4' 11-1/2"	Polished Ivory	9,560.
SG-150CKAF	4' 11-1/2"	French Provincial—All Finishes	11,190.
SG-150CKBF	4' 11-1/2"	French Provincial—All Finishes	12,050.
SG-161	5' 3-1/2"	Wood Finishes and Pol. Wood Finishes	11,640.
SG-161	5' 3-1/2"	Polished White	11,120.
SG-161	5' 3-1/2"	Polished Ivory	11,120.
SG-161KAF	5' 3-1/2"	French Provincial—All Finishes	12,860.
SG-161KBF	5' 3-1/2"	French Provincial—All Finishes	13,260.
SG-172	5' 7"	Ebony and Polished Ebony	11,990.
SG-172	5' 7"	Wood Finishes and Pol. Wood Finishes	12,500.
SG-172	5' 7"	Polished White	11,990.
SG-172	5' 7"	Polished Ivory	11,990.
SG-172L	5' 7"	Empire Ebony and Polished Ebony	13,060.
SG-172L	5' 7"	Empire Wood Finishes	13,580.
SG-172L	5' 7"	Empire Polished White	13,580.
SG-172L	5' 7"	Empire Polished Ivory	13,580.
SG-185	6' 1"	Ebony and Polished Ebony	12,840.
SG-185	6' 1"	Wood Finishes	13,360.
SG-185	6' 1"	Polished White	13,360.
SG-185	6' 1"	Polished Ivory	13,360.
SG-185L	6' 1"	Empire Ebony and Polished Ebony	13,920.
SG-185L	6' 1"	Empire Wood Finishes	14,430.
SG-185L	6' 1"	Empire Polished White	14,430.
SG-185L	6' 1"	Empire Polished Ivory	14,430.
All grands	—	*Rosewood or Bubinga Finish, add'l*	1,000.

Model	Size	Style and Finish	Price*

Sängler & Söhne / Wieler

Verticals

Model	Size	Style and Finish	Price*
C43R	43"	Oak (round leg)	3,100.
C43R	43"	Mahogany (round leg)	3,100.
C43F	43"	French Oak	3,100.
C43F	43"	French Mahogany	3,100.
111GD	44"	Continental Polished Ebony	2,620.
111GD	44"	Continental Polished Mahogany	2,680.
111GD	44"	Continental Polished Walnut	2,680.
111GD	44"	Continental Polished White	2,680.
115GC	45"	Chippendale Polished Ebony	2,880.
115GC	45"	Chippendale Polished Mahogany	2,920.
115GC	45"	Chippendale Polished Brown Mahogany	2,920.
450	45"	Italian Provincial Walnut	3,340.
450	45"	Italian Provincial Mahogany	3,340.
450	45"	Italian Provincial Cherry	3,340.
451	45"	Walnut (round leg)	3,340.
451	45"	Mahogany (round leg)	3,340.
451	45"	Cherry (round leg)	3,340.
452	45"	French Walnut	3,340.
452	45"	French Mahogany	3,340.
452	45"	French Oak	3,340.
452	45"	French Cherry	3,340.
115WH	46"	Polished Ebony	2,920.
115WH	46"	Polished Mahogany	2,970.
115WH	46"	Polished Walnut	2,970.
121WH	48"	Polished Ebony	3,140.
121WH	48"	Polished Mahogany	3,250.
121WH	48"	Polished Walnut	3,250.
131X	52"	Polished Ebony	4,190.
131X	52"	Polished Mahogany	4,390.

Grands

Model	Size	Style and Finish	Price*
450	4' 7"	Polished Ebony	9,000.
450	4' 7"	Polished Mahogany	9,360.
450	4' 7"	Polished Brown Oak	9,360.
148SR	4' 11"	Victorian Polished Ebony	9,390.

*For explanation of terms and prices, please see pages 28–33.

Model	Size	Style and Finish	Price*

Sängler & Söhne / Wieler (continued)

Model	Size	Style and Finish	Price*
148SR	4' 11"	Victorian Polished Mahogany	9,390.
148SR	4' 11"	Victorian Polished Walnut	9,390.
152DP	5'	Polished Ebony	8,390.
152DP	5'	Polished Mahogany	8,790.
152DP	5'	Polished Walnut	8,790.
152DP	5'	Polished White	8,790.
480	5' 1"	Polished Ebony	10,350.
480	5' 1"	Polished Mahogany	10,720.
165DP	5' 4"	Polished Ebony	9,100.
165DP	5' 4"	Polished Mahogany	9,700.
165DP	5' 4"	Polished Walnut	9,700.
165DP	5' 4"	Polished White	9,700.
185DP	6' 1"	Polished Ebony	10,390.
185DP	6' 1"	Polished Mahogany	10,790.

Sauter

Verticals

Model	Size	Style and Finish	Price*
122	48"	"Schulpiano" Beech	13,500.
122	48"	"Domino" Polished Ebony	15,880.
122	48"	"Domino" Pear	15,880.
122	48"	"Resonance" Cherry/Yew	17,950.
122	48"	"Vista" Polished Ebony	17,170.
122	48"	"Vista" Maple	16,300.
122	48"	"Vista" Pear	17,880.
122	48"	"Vista" Cherry	17,400.
122	48"	"M-Line M2" Polished Ebony	20,900.
128	50"	"M-Line M1" Polished Ebony	24,450.
130	51"	"Competence" Polished Ebony	19,800.

Grands

Model	Size	Style and Finish	Price*
160	5' 3"	"Alpha" Polished Ebony	41,900.
160	5' 3"	"Alpha" Walnut	38,000.
160	5' 3"	"Alpha" Mahogany	38,000.
160	5' 3"	"Alpha" Polished White	43,250.
160	5' 3"	Chippendale Walnut	41,400.

Model	Size	Style and Finish	Price*
160	5' 3"	Chippendale Mahogany	41,400.
160	5' 3"	Chippendale Cherry	44,700.
160	5' 3"	"Noblesse" Walnut	42,800.
160	5' 3"	"Noblesse" Mahogany	42,800.
160	5' 3"	"Noblesse" Cherry	46,100.
185	6' 1"	"Delta" Polished Ebony	45,750.
185	6' 1"	"Delta" Walnut	41,920.
185	6' 1"	"Delta" Mahogany	41,920.
185	6' 1"	Chippendale Walnut	46,720.
185	6' 1"	Chippendale Mahogany	46,720.
185	6' 1"	Chippendale Cherry	50,020.
185	6' 1"	"Noblesse" Walnut	48,920.
185	6' 1"	"Noblesse" Mahogany	48,920.
185	6' 1"	"Noblesse" Cherry	50,520.
220	7' 2"	"Omega" Polished Ebony	58,500.
220	7' 2"	"Omega" Walnut	54,900.
220	7' 2"	"Omega" Mahogany	54,900.
275	9'	"Concert" Polished Ebony	99,590.
Satin models		*Additional, for polished finish*	5,400.
Peter Maly models		*Available by special order only*	on request

Schimmel

Verticals

112 S	45"	"School" Open-Pore Ebony	12.980.
112 S	45"	"School" Open-Pore Walnut	12,980.
112 S	45"	"School" Open-Pore Oak	12,980.
116 E	46"	"Exquisite" Polished Ebony	12,780.
116 E	46"	"Exquisite" Polished Mahogany	13,180.
116 E	46"	*"Exquisite" Polished White*	13,180.
116 E	46"	"Exquisite" Alder	13,180.
116 E	46"	"Exquisite" Open-Pore Walnut	13,180.
116 E	46"	"Exquisite" Open-Pore Beech	13,180.
116 E	46"	"Exquisite" Open-Pore Maple	13,180.
116 E	46"	"Exquisite" Open-Pore Ash	13,180.
116 E	46"	"Exquisite" Waxed Plum	13,180.
116 E	46"	"Exquisite" O.P. Waxed Swiss Pear	13,180.

*For explanation of terms and prices, please see pages 28–33.

Model	Size	Style and Finish	Price*

Schimmel (continued)

Model	Size	Style and Finish	Price*
116 S	46"	"Special" Polished Ebony	11,980.
116 S	46"	"Special" Alder	12,780.
116 S	46"	"Special" Open-Pore Walnut	12,780.
116 S	46"	"Special" Open-Pore Birch	12,780.
116 S	46"	"Special" Open-Pore Beech	12,780.
116 S	46"	"Special" Waxed Swiss Pear	12,780.
120 I	48"	"International" Polished Ebony	13,180.
120 I	48"	"International" Polished Mahogany	13,580.
120 I	48"	*"International" Polished White*	13,580.
120 J	48"	"Centennial" Pol. Mahog. with Myrtle Inlay	13,980.
120 J	48"	"Centennial" Pol. Cherry with Yew Inlay	14,380.
120 LE	48"	"Lyra Exquisite" Polished Ebony	13,580.
120 LE	48"	"Lyra Exquisite" Polished Mahogany	13,980.
120 M	48"	"Solid" Open-Pore Waxed Maple	14,980.
120 RI	48"	"Royale Intarsia" Polished Mahogany	15,580.
120 RI	48"	*"Royale Intarsia" Polished Cherry*	15,980.
120 S	48"	"School" Open-Pore Ebony	13,380.
120 S	48"	"School" Open-Pore Oak	13,380.
120 TN	48"	"Noblesse" Polished Ebony	13,580.
120 TN	48"	*"Noblesse" Polished White*	13,980.
120 TN-SE	48"	"Noblesse" Sig. Ed. Polished Ebony	13,980.
120 TR	48"	"Residence" Polished Ebony	13,580.
120 TR	48"	"Residence" Polished Mahogany	13,980.
122 KE	49"	"Classicism Exquisite" Polished Ebony	13,780.
122 KE	49"	"Classicism Exquisite" Pol. Mahogany	14,180.
122 KE	49"	*"Classicism Exquisite" O.P. Waxed Alder*	14,580.
122 KE	49"	*"Classicism Exquisite" Polished Cherry*	14,580.
F 122 AC	49"	"Art Cubus" Polished Ebony	15,500.
F 122 AC	49"	"Art Cubus" Waxed Swiss Pear	15,900.
F 122 SE	49"	"Salon Exquisite" Polished Ebony	14,700.
F 122 SE	49"	"Salon Exquisite" Waxed Swiss Pear	15,100.
S 125 DN	49"	"Diamond Noblesse" Polished Ebony	17,180.
S 125 DN	49"	"Diamond Noblesse" Polished Mahog.	17,580.
S 125 DP	49"	"Diamond Prestige" Polished Ebony	17,580.
S 125 DP	49"	"Diamond Prestige" Pol. Mahogany	17,980.

Model	Size	Style and Finish	Price*
130 T	51"	Polished Ebony	15,780.
130 T	51"	Polished Mahogany	16,180.
130 T	51"	*Polished Walnut*	16,180.
130 T	51"	*Polished White*	16,180.
130 T-O	51"	Polished Ebony (upper panel oval inlay)	16,180.
O 132 DT	52"	"Diamond Tradition" Polished Ebony	18,200.
O 132 DT	52"	"Diamond Tradition" Pol. Mahogany	18,800.

Grands

When not mentioned, satin finish available on special order at same price as high-polish finish.

GP 169 T	5' 7"	Polished Ebony	33,980.
SP 182 C	6'	*Chippendale Polished Walnut*	38,980.
SP 182 C	6'	*Chippendale Polished Mahogany*	38,980.
SP 182 DE	6'	"Diamond Edition" Polished Ebony	38,980.
SP 182 DE	6'	"Diamond Edition" Polished White	42,380.
SP 182 DE	6'	"Diamond Edition" Pol. Pyramid Mahog.	42,380.
SP 182 DE	6'	"Diamond Edition" Polished Bubinga	42,380.
SP 182 DE	6'	*"Diamond Edition" Pol. Bird's Eye Maple*	42,380.
SP 182 DE	6'	*"Diamond Edition" Pol. Swiss Pear*	42,380.
SP 182 DE	6'	"Diamond Edition" Macassar	42,380.
SP 182 E	6'	Empire Polished Pyramid Mahogany	43,980.
SP 182 S	6'	"School" Open-Pore Oak	34,780.
SP 182 T	6'	Polished Ebony	35,580.
SP 182 T	6'	Polished Walnut	36,380.
SP 182 T	6'	Polished Mahogany	36,380.
SP 182 T	6'	Polished White	36,380.
SP 182 TE	6'	"Exquisite" Polished Ebony	37,180.
SP 182 TE	6'	"Exquisite" Polished Mahogany	37,980.
SP 182 TE	6'	*"Exquisite" Polished White*	37,980.
SP 182 TE-I	6'	"Exquisite" Polished Mahogany Intarsia	38,980.
SP 182 TJ	6'	"Jubilee" Polished Ebony	37,580.
SP 182 TJ	6'	"Jubilee" Polished Mahogany	38,380.
SP 182 TJ	6'	*"Jubilee" Polished White*	38,380.
SP 182 TJ	6'	*"Jubilee" Polished Swiss Pear*	38,380.
208 P	7'	*"Pegasus" Acrylic*	169,800.
CC 213 A	7'	*"Art Edition"*	119,800.
CC 213 C	7'	*Chippendale Polished Mahogany*	44,580.

*For explanation of terms and prices, please see pages 28–33.

Model	Size	Style and Finish	Price*

Schimmel (continued)

Model	Size	Style and Finish	Price*
CC 213 C	7'	*Chippendale Polished Walnut*	44,580.
CC 213 DE	7'	"Diamond Edition" Polished Ebony	44,580.
CC 213 DE	7'	*"Diamond Edition" Polished White*	47,980.
CC 213 DE	7'	"Diamond Edition" Pol. Pyramid Mahog.	47,980.
CC 213 DE	7'	"Diamond Edition" Polished Bubinga	47,980.
CC 213 DE	7'	*"Diamond Edition" Pol. Bird's Eye Maple*	47,980.
CC 213 DE	7'	*"Diamond Edition" Pol. Swiss Pear*	47,980.
CC 213 DE	7'	"Diamond Edition" Macassar	47,980.
CC 213 G	7'	*Plexiglass Clear Acrylic*	99,800.
CC 213 S	7'	"School" Open-Pore Oak	40,380.
CC 213 T	7'	Polished Ebony	41,180.
CC 213 T	7'	Polished Mahogany	41,980.
CC 213 T	7'	*Polished White*	41,980.
CC 213 T	7'	*Polished Walnut*	41,980.
CC 213 TE	7'	"Exquisite" Polished Ebony	42,780.
CC 213 TE	7'	*"Exquisite" Polished Mahogany*	43,580.
CC 213 TE	7'	*"Exquisite" Polished White*	43,580.
CC 213 TJ	7'	"Jubilee" Polished Ebony	43,180.
CC 213 TJ	7'	*"Jubilee" Polished Mahogany*	43,980.
CC 213 TJ	7'	*"Jubilee" Polished White*	43,980.
CC 213 TJ	7'	*"Jubilee" Polished Swiss Pear*	43,980.
CO 256 T	8' 4"	Polished Ebony	63,800.

Schubert

Verticals

Model	Size	Style and Finish	Price*
B-21	43"	Continental Polished Ebony	2,250.
B-21	43"	Continental Polished Cherry	2,280.
B-21	43"	Continental Polished Oak	2,250.
B-20	44"	Country French Oak	2,480.
B-20	44"	French Provincial Mahogany	2,480.
B-22	44"	Polished Ebony	2,490.
B-22	44"	Polished Mahogany	2,490.
B-22	44"	Polished Oak	2,490.
B-23	44"	Chippendale Polished Ebony	2,590.

Model	Size	Style and Finish	Price*
B-23	44"	Chippendale Polished Mahogany	2,590.
B-23	44"	Chippendale Polished Walnut	2,590.
B-23	44"	Chippendale Oak	2,590.
B-23	44"	Chippendale Polished Oak	2,590.
B-23	44"	Chippendale Polished Cherry	2,590.
B-7-R	46"	Continental Polished Mahogany	1,990.
B-15-A	47"	Polished Ebony	2,590.
B-15-A	47"	Polished Mahogany	2,590.
B-15-A	47"	Polished Walnut	2,590.
B-15-A	47"	Polished Oak	2,590.

Schultz & Sons

Model numbers beginning with 3 or 4 designate pianos manufactured by Broadwood, numbers beginning with 7 or 8, by Samick.

Verticals

Model	Size	Style and Finish	Price
3807-S	47"	Polished Ebony	20,050.
3807-S	47"	Walnut	18,995.
3807-S	47"	Polished Walnut	21,295.
3807-S	47"	Mahogany	18,995.
3807-S	47"	Polished Mahogany	21,295.
3809-S	47"	Mahogany	25,250.
3809-S	47"	Polished Mahogany	26,295.
3819-S	47"	Walnut	21,495.
3819-S	47"	Polished Walnut	23,595.
3819-S	47"	Mahogany	21,495.
3819-S	47"	Polished Mahogany	23,595.
7708-S	47-1/2"	Polished Mahogany	10,995.
7708-S	47-1/2"	Polished Cherry	10,995.
7708-SCC	47-1/2"	*Custom Finish*	14,150.
7703-S	47-1/2"	Polished Mahogany	10,995.
7703-S	47-1/2"	Polished Cherry	10,995.
7703-SCC	47-1/2"	*Custom Finish*	14,150.
7707-U	48-1/2"	Ebony and Polished Ebony	11,750.
7707-U	48-1/2"	Walnut and Polished Walnut	12,650.
7707-U	48-1/2"	Polished Mahogany	12,650.
3817-U	50"	Polished Ebony	26,295.

*For explanation of terms and prices, please see pages 28–33.

Model	Size	Style and Finish	Price*

Schultz & Sons (continued)

Model	Size	Style and Finish	Price*
3817-U	50"	Walnut	24,650.
3817-U	50"	Polished Walnut	27,595.
3817-U	50"	Mahogany	24,650.
3817-U	50"	Polished Mahogany	27,595.
7717-U	52"	Ebony and Polished Ebony	12,650.
7717-U	52"	Walnut and Polished Walnut	13,450.
7717-U	52"	Polished Mahogany	13,450.

Grands

Model	Size	Style and Finish	Price*
8501-B	5' 2"	Ebony and Polished Ebony	18,850.
8501-B	5' 2"	Walnut and Polished Walnut	19,250.
8501-B	5' 2"	Polished Mahogany	19,250.
8501-B	5' 2"	Polished Ivory	19,295.
8501-B	5' 2"	Polished White	19,295.
8601-B	5' 2"	Ebony and Polished Ebony	26,850.
8601-B	5' 2"	Walnut and Polished Walnut	27,750.
8601-B	5' 2"	Polished Mahogany	27,750.
8601-B	5' 2"	Polished Ivory	26,950.
8601-B	5' 2"	Polished White	26,950.
8601-M	5' 9-1/2"	"Classic" Ebony and Polished Ebony	21,195.
8601-M	5' 9-1/2"	"Classic" Walnut and Polished Walnut	22,250.
8601-M	5' 9-1/2"	"Classic" Polished Mahogany	22,250.
8601-M	5' 9-1/2"	"Classic" Polished Ivory	21,750.
8601-M	5' 9-1/2"	"Classic" Polished White	21,750.
8701-M	5' 9-1/2"	"Classic" Ebony and Polished Ebony	28,250.
8701-M	5' 9-1/2"	"Classic" Walnut and Polished Walnut	29,195.
8701-M	5' 9-1/2"	"Classic" Polished Mahogany	29,195.
8701-M	5' 9-1/2"	"Classic" Polished Ivory	28,750.
8701-M	5' 9-1/2"	"Classic" Polished White	28,750.
8721-M	5' 9-1/2"	"Victorian" Ebony and Polished Ebony	23,450.
8721-M	5' 9-1/2"	"Victorian" Walnut and Pol. Walnut	24,595.
8721-M	5' 9-1/2"	"Victorian" Polished Mahogany	24,595.
8721-M	5' 9-1/2"	"Victorian" Polished Ivory	24,095.
8721-M	5' 9-1/2"	"Victorian" Polished White	24,095.
8821-M	5' 9-1/2"	"Victorian" Ebony and Polished Ebony	30,695.
8821-M	5' 9-1/2"	"Victorian" Walnut and Pol. Walnut	31,650.

Model	Size	Style and Finish	Price*
8821-M	5' 9-1/2"	"Victorian" Polished Mahogany	31,650.
8821-M	5' 9-1/2"	"Victorian" Polished Ivory	30,895.
8821-M	5' 9-1/2"	"Victorian" Polished White	30,895.
8741-M	5' 9-1/2"	Polished Mahogany with Floral Inlays	29,795.
8741-MCC	5' 9-1/2"	*Custom Finish with Floral Inlays*	36,850.
8741-MCS	5' 9-1/2"	*Custom Finish with Custom Inlays*	on request
8731-M	5' 9-1/2"	Louis XV Ebony and Polished Ebony	26,750.
8731-M	5' 9-1/2"	Louis XV Walnut and Polished Walnut	27,750.
8731-M	5' 9-1/2"	Louis XV Polished Mahogany	27,750.
8731-M	5' 9-1/2"	Louis XV Polished Ivory	27,250.
8731-M	5' 9-1/2"	Louis XV Polished White	27,250.
4908-L	6'	"Euro Classic" Ebony	72,495.
4908-L	6'	"Euro Classic" Polished Ebony	74,995.
8701-L	6' 1"	"Classic" Ebony and Polished Ebony	22,695.
8701-L	6' 1"	"Classic" Walnut and Polished Walnut	23,595.
8701-L	6' 1"	"Classic" Polished Mahogany	23,595.
8701-L	6' 1"	"Classic" Polished Ivory	22,995.
8701-L	6' 1"	"Classic" Polished White	22,995.
8801-L	6' 1"	"Classic" Ebony and Polished Ebony	29,850.
8801-L	6' 1"	"Classic" Walnut and Polished Walnut	30,795.
8801-L	6' 1"	"Classic" Polished Mahogany	30,795.
8801-L	6' 1"	"Classic" Polished Ivory	30,095.
8801-L	6' 1"	"Classic" Polished White	30,095.
8709-L	6' 1"	"Victorian" Ebony and Polished Ebony	24,995.
8709-L	6' 1"	"Victorian" Walnut and Pol. Walnut	26,195.
8709-L	6' 1"	"Victorian" Polished Mahogany	26,195.
8709-L	6' 1"	"Victorian" Polished Ivory	25,495.
8709-L	6' 1"	"Victorian" Polished White	25,495.
8809-L	6' 1"	"Victorian" Ebony and Polished Ebony	32,895.
8809-L	6' 1"	"Victorian" Walnut and Pol. Walnut	33,995.
8809-L	6' 1"	"Victorian" Polished Mahogany	33,995.
8809-L	6' 1"	"Victorian" Polished Ivory	34,150.
8809-L	6' 1"	"Victorian" Polished White	34,150.
8811-X	6' 9"	Ebony and Polished Ebony	40,350.
8811-SX	7' 1"	Ebony and Polished Ebony	45,350.

*For explanation of terms and prices, please see pages 28–33.

Schulze Pollmann

Verticals

Model	Size	Style and Finish	Price*
113	45"	Polished Ebony	8,390.
113	45"	Polished Peacock Ebony	9,190.
113	45"	Polished Briar Mahogany	9,190.
113	45"	Polished Peacock Mahogany	9,190.
113	45"	Polished Briar Walnut	9,190.
113	45"	Polished Peacock Walnut	9,190.
118/P8	46"	Polished Ebony	10,190.
118/P8	46"	Polished Briar Walnut	11,590.
118/P8	46"	Polished Feather Mahogany	11,590.
126/P6	50"	Polished Ebony	12,790.
126/P6	50"	Polished Peacock Ebony	13,790.
126/P6	50"	Polished Peacock Cherry	13,790.
126/P6	50"	Oval Feather Mahogany	13,790.
126/P6	50"	Polished Mahogany	13,790.
126/P6	50"	Polished Briar Mahogany	13,790.
126/P6	50"	Polished Peacock Mahogany	13,790.
126/P6	50"	Polished Sunburst Mahogany	13,790.
126/P6	50"	Polished Briar Walnut	13,790.
126/P6	50"	Satin and Polished Peacock Walnut	13,790.
126/P6	50"	Polished Sunburst Walnut	13,790.

Grands

Model	Size	Style and Finish	Price*
160GK	5' 3"	Polished Ebony	25,990.
160GK	5' 3"	Polished Walnut	27,790.
160GK	5' 3"	Polished Briar Walnut	28,790.
160GK	5' 3"	Polished Mahogany	27,790.
160GK	5' 3"	Polished Briar Mahogany	28,790.
160GK	5' 3"	Polished Ebony (round leg)	27,590.
160GK	5' 3"	Polished Walnut (round leg)	29,190.
160GK	5' 3"	Polished Mahogany (round leg)	29,190.
160GK	5' 3"	Chippendale Polished Walnut	32,590.
160GK	5' 3"	Chippendale Polished Mahogany	32,590.
160GK	5' 3"	With Renner Action, add'l	2,800.
190F	6' 2"	Polished Ebony	37,390.
190F	6' 2"	Polished Mahogany	39,990.

Model	Size	Style and Finish	Price*
190F	6' 2"	Polished Briar Mahogany	42,390.
190F	6' 2"	Polished Walnut	39,990.
190F	6' 2"	Polished Briar Walnut	42,390.
197A	6' 7"	Polished Ebony	44,990.
197A	6' 7"	Polished Briar Mahogany	49,990.
197A	6' 7"	Polished Briar Walnut	49,990.

Seidl & Sohn

Prices do not include bench.

Verticals

SL 109	43"	Continental Polished Ebony	6,526.
SL 109	43"	Continental Polished Walnut	6,526.
SL 109	43"	Continental Polished Flame Mahogany	6,526.
SL 109	43"	Continental Polished White	6,673.
SL 113	46"	Polished Ebony	6,694.
SL 113	46"	Polished Walnut	6,694.
SL 113	46"	Polished Flame Mahogany	6,694.
SL 113	46"	Polished White	6,841.
SL 117	47"	Chippendale Polished Walnut	7,259.
SL 117	47"	Chippendale Polished Mahogany	7,259.
SL 120	48"	Polished Ebony	7,050.
SL 120	48"	Polished Walnut	7,050.
SL 120	48"	Polished Flame Mahogany	7,050.
SL 120	48"	Polished White	7,217.
SL 127	51"	Polished Ebony	8,076.
SL 127	51"	Polished Walnut	8,076.
SL 127	51"	Polished Mahogany	8,076.
SL 120/127		*Renner Action, add'l*	639.

Seiler

Verticals

116	46"	"Mondial" Open-Pore Ebony	13,840.
116	46"	"Mondial" Open-Pore Walnut	13,840.
116	46"	"Mondial" Open-Pore Mahogany	13,840.
116	46"	"Mondial" Polished Mahogany	14,480.

*For explanation of terms and prices, please see pages 28–33.

Model	Size	Style and Finish	Price*
Seiler (continued)			
116	46"	"Mondial" Open-Pore Oak	13,840.
116	46"	"Mondial" Open-Pore Maple	13,840.
116	46"	"Mondial" Open-Pore Cherry	14,480.
116	46"	"Mondial" Alderwood	13,960.
116	46"	"Mondial" Open-Pore Swiss Pear	14,280.
116	46"	"Mondial" Open-Pore Apple Heartwood	15,020.
116	46"	"Jubilee" Polished Ebony	14,840.
116	46"	"Jubilee" Polished White	15,080.
116	46"	Chippendale Open-Pore Walnut	13,960.
116	46"	"Escorial" Open-Pore Cherry, Intarsia	15,080.
122	48"	"Konsole" Open-Pore Ebony	14,400.
122	48"	"Konsole" Polished Ebony	15,380.
122	48"	"Konsole" Open-Pore Walnut	14,400.
122	48"	"Konsole" Polished Walnut Rootwood	20,820.
122	48"	"Konsole" Open-Pore Oak	14,400.
122	48"	"Konsole" Open-Pore Maple	14,400.
122	48"	"Konsole" Maple Burl	14,980.
122	48"	"Konsole" Open-Pore Cherry	15,100.
122	48"	"Konsole" Polished Burl Rosewood	17,780.
122	48"	"Konsole" Polished Brown Ash	17,780.
122	48"	"Konsole" Polished Redwood Burl	18,420.
122	48"	"Konsole" Polished White	15,780.
122	48"	"School" Open-Pore Ebony	13,740.
122	48"	"School" Open-Pore Walnut	13,740.
122	48"	"School" Open-Pore Oak	13,740.
122	48"	"Vienna" Polished Ebony w/Pilaster	15,780.
122	48"	"Vienna" Pol. Ebony w/Pilaster & Oval	15,960.
122	48"	"Vienna" Pol. Mahog. w/ Flower Inlays	17,780.
122	48"	"Vienna" Pol. Walnut w/ Flower Inlays	17,780.
122	48"	"Vienna" Maple with Pilaster	15,780.
122	48"	"Vienna" Maple with Pilaster & Oval	15,960.
132	52"	"Concert SMR" Polished Ebony	19,580.
132	52"	"Concert SMR" Pol. Ebony w/Oval	20,160.
132	52"	"Concert SMR" Pol. Ebony w/Candle	20,140.
132	52"	"Concert SMR" Pol. Ebony w/Panels	20,280.

Model	Size	Style and Finish	Price*
132	52"	"Concert SMR" Open-Pore Walnut	19,000.
132	52"	"Concert SMR" Polished Mahogany	20,180.
132	52"	"Limited Edition" Polished Ebony	22,580.
132	52"	"Lim. Edit." Pol. Eb. w/Oval or Pilaster	23,040.
132	52"	"Lim. Edit." Pol. Eb. w/Oval & Pilaster	23,500.

Grands

Model	Size	Style and Finish	Price*
180	5' 11"	"Maestro" Polished Ebony	40,480.
180	5' 11"	"Maestro" Open-Pore Walnut	40,480.
180	5' 11"	"Maestro" Polished Walnut	43,200.
180	5' 11"	"Maestro" Open-Pore Mahogany	40,480.
180	5' 11"	"Maestro" Polished Mahogany	43,200.
180	5' 11"	"Maestro" Polished Pyramid Mahogany	56,720.
180	5' 11"	"Maestro" Polished Burl Rosewood	50,560.
180	5' 11"	"Maestro" Polished Maple	56,720.
180	5' 11"	"Maestro" Polished White	41,400.
180	5' 11"	Chippendale Open-Pore Walnut	43,100.
180	5' 11"	"Westminster" Pol. Mahogany, Intarsia	56,720.
180	5' 11"	"Florenz" Pol. Walnut/Myrtle, Intarsia	56,720.
180	5' 11"	"Florenz" Pol. Mahog./Myrtle, Intarsia	56,720.
180	5' 11"	"Louvre" Polished Ebony	45,480.
180	5' 11"	"Louvre" Polished Cherry, Intarsia	56,720.
180	5' 11"	"Louvre" Polished White	46,260.
180	5' 11"	"Prado" Polished Brown Ash	58,320.
180	5' 11"	"Prado" Polished Burl Redwood	60,400.
180	5' 11"	"Stella" Pol. Maple Rootwood, Intarsia	69,660.
180	5' 11"	"Meridian" Pol. Maple Rootwood Intarsia	69,660.
180	5' 11"	"Concordia" Pol. Maple Rootwood Intarsia	69,660.
180	5' 11"	"Showmaster" Chrome/Brass/Polyester	112,980.
180	5' 11"	"Suspension"	150,800.
206	6' 9"	Polished Ebony	45,580.
208	6' 10"	Polished Ebony	50,840.
208	6' 10"	"Empire 1897" Open-Pore Blue w/Brass	157,240.
208	6' 10"	"Solitaire" Custom with Painting	177,240.
208	6' 10"	"Solitaire" Custom without Painting	143,880.
242	8' 1"	Polished Ebony	69,100.

*For explanation of terms and prices, please see pages 28–33.

Model	Size	Style and Finish	Price*

Steinberg, Wilh.

Verticals

Model	Size	Style and Finish	Price*
IQ 16	46"	Polished Ebony	9,300.
IQ 16	46"	Polished Ebony with Trim	9,700.
IQ 16	46"	Polished Ebony with Oval Inlay	9,800.
IQ 16	46"	Polished Mahogany	9,640.
IQ 16	46"	Polished Mahogany with Inlay	9,975.
IQ 16	46"	Polished Walnut	9,640.
IQ 16	46"	Polished Oak	9,640.
IQ 16	46"	Polished Cherry	9,640.
IQ 16	46"	"Amadeus" Polished Ebony	9,710.
C 2	48"	Polished Ebony	9,150.
C 2	48"	Mahogany and Polished Mahogany	9,550.
IQ 22	49"	Polished Ebony	10,090.
IQ-22	49"	Polished Ebony with Trim	10,500.
IQ 22	49"	Polished Mahogany	10,895.
IQ 22	49"	Polished Walnut	10,895.
IQ 22	49"	Polished Cherry	10,895.
IQ 22	49"	"Amadeus" Polished Ebony	11,350.
IQ 28	52"	Polished Ebony	12,850.
IQ 28	52"	Polished Ebony with Trim	13,250.
IQ 28	52"	Polished Walnut	13,050.
IQ 28	52"	Polished Oak	13,050.
IQ 28	52"	Polished Cherry	13,050.
IQ 28	52"	"Amadeus" Polished Ebony	13,450.
IQ 28	52"	"Passione" Polished Ebony	14,650.
IQ 28	52"	"Passione" Polished Ebony with Trim	14,850.

Grands

Model	Size	Style and Finish	Price*
IQ 77	5' 9"	Polished Ebony	33,060.
IQ 77	5' 9"	Polished Mahogany	34,060.
IQ 77	5' 9"	Polished Mahogany with Inlay	36,000.
IQ 77	5' 9"	Polished Walnut	34,060.
IQ 99	6' 3"	Polished Ebony	39,000.
IQ 99	6' 3"	Polished Mahogany	40,500.
IQ 99	6' 3"	Polished Mahogany with Inlay	42,500.
IQ 99	6' 3"	Polished Walnut	40,500.

Steingraeber & Söhne

This list includes only those models most likely to be offered to U.S. customers. Other models, styles, and finishes are available.

Verticals

Model	Size	Style and Finish	Price
122T	48"	French Cherry with Ebony Accents	21,800.
130PS	51"	Polished Ebony with "Twist" Panels	29,780.
130K	51"	"Classicism" Polished Ebony	27,400.
130K	51"	"Classicism" Walnut	25,500.
138K	54"	Polished Ebony	31,780.

Grands

Model	Size	Style and Finish	Price
168N	5' 6"	Polished Ebony	47,700.
168K	5' 6"	"Classicism" Polished Ebony	56,530.
168K	5' 6"	"Classicism" Pol. Ebony w/Mahogany	63,500.
168K	5' 6"	"Classicism" Pol. Ebony w/Burl Walnut	63,500.
168C	5' 6"	Chippendale French Walnut	61,800.
205N	6' 9"	Polished Ebony	64,490.
205N	6' 9"	Polished Ebony with Burl Trim	66,200.
205K	6' 9"	"Classicism" Polished Ebony	72,880.

Steinway & Sons

Verticals

Model	Size	Style and Finish	Price
4510	45"	Sheraton Ebony	18,500.
4510	45"	Sheraton Mahogany	20,400.
4510	45"	Sheraton Walnut	21,100.
4510	45"	Sheraton Dark Cherry	21,700.
1098	46-1/2"	Ebony	17,600.
1098	46-1/2"	Mahogany	18,800.
1098	46-1/2"	Walnut	19,500.
K-52	52"	Ebony	23,000.
K-52	52"	Mahogany	25,900.
K-52	52"	Walnut	26,600.

Grands

Model	Size	Style and Finish	Price
S	5' 1"	Ebony	37,800.
S	5' 1"	Mahogany	42,200.
S	5' 1"	Walnut	43,500.

*For explanation of terms and prices, please see pages 28–33.

Model	Size	Style and Finish	Price*

Steinway & Sons (continued)

Model	Size	Style and Finish	Price*
S	5' 1"	Figured Sapele	45,900.
S	5' 1"	Dark Cherry	46,200.
S	5' 1"	Kewazinga Bubinga	47,100.
S	5' 1"	African Cherry	48,900.
S	5' 1"	Satinwood	51,800.
S	5' 1"	Santos Rosewood	52,500.
S	5' 1"	Pearwood	52,800.
S	5' 1"	East Indian Rosewood	53,500.
S	5' 1"	African Pommele	53,900.
S	5' 1"	Macassar Ebony	59,000.
S	5' 1"	Hepplewhite Dark Cherry	47,300.
M	5' 7"	Ebony	41,000.
M	5' 7"	Mahogany	45,900.
M	5' 7"	Walnut	47,100.
M	5' 7"	Figured Sapele	49,100.
M	5' 7"	Dark Cherry	49,500.
M	5' 7"	Kewazinga Bubinga	51,500.
M	5' 7"	African Cherry	52,200.
M	5' 7"	Satinwood	55,100.
M	5' 7"	Santos Rosewood	56,600.
M	5' 7"	Pearwood	57,000.
M	5' 7"	East Indian Rosewood	57,600.
M	5' 7"	African Pommele	57,900.
M	5' 7"	Macassar Ebony	63,400.
M	5' 7"	Hepplewhite Dark Cherry	51,700.
M 1014A	5' 7"	Chippendale Mahogany	56,000.
M 1014A	5' 7"	Chippendale Walnut	57,400.
M 501A	5' 7"	Louis XV Walnut	73,200.
M 501A	5' 7"	Louis XV East Indian Rosewood	85,000.
L	5' 10-1/2"	Ebony	45,700.
L	5' 10-1/2"	Mahogany	51,500.
L	5' 10-1/2"	Walnut	52,500.
L	5' 10-1/2"	Figured Sapele	54,800.
L	5' 10-1/2"	Dark Cherry	55,700.
L	5' 10-1/2"	Kewazinga Bubinga	57,600.

Model	Size	Style and Finish	Price*
L	5' 10-1/2"	African Cherry	58,700.
L	5' 10-1/2"	Satinwood	60,300.
L	5' 10-1/2"	Santos Rosewood	64,100.
L	5' 10-1/2"	Pearwood	64,500.
L	5' 10-1/2"	East Indian Rosewood	65,100.
L	5' 10-1/2"	African Pommele	65,400.
L	5' 10-1/2"	Macassar Ebony	71,200.
L	5' 10-1/2"	Hepplewhite Dark Cherry	58,000.
A	6' 2"	Limited Edition Tricentennial Pol. Eby.	75,700.
B	6' 10-1/2"	Ebony	57,900.
B	6' 10-1/2"	Mahogany	65,100.
B	6' 10-1/2"	Walnut	66,500.
B	6' 10-1/2"	Figured Sapele	69,600.
B	6' 10-1/2"	Dark Cherry	70,900.
B	6' 10-1/2"	Kewazinga Bubinga	72,800.
B	6' 10-1/2"	African Cherry	73,200.
B	6' 10-1/2"	Satinwood	73,600.
B	6' 10-1/2"	Santos Rosewood	80,900.
B	6' 10-1/2"	Pearwood	81,300.
B	6' 10-1/2"	East Indian Rosewood	82,100.
B	6' 10-1/2"	African Pommele	82,500.
B	6' 10-1/2"	Macassar Ebony	89,600.
B	6' 10-1/2"	Hepplewhite Dark Cherry	73,600.
D	8' 11-3/4"	Ebony	86,400.
D	8' 11-3/4"	Mahogany	94,600.
D	8' 11-3/4"	Walnut	96,100.
D	8' 11-3/4"	Figured Sapele	100,500.
D	8' 11-3/4"	Dark Cherry	102,300.
D	8' 11-3/4"	Kewazinga Bubinga	104,600.
D	8' 11-3/4"	African Cherry	107,100.
D	8' 11-3/4"	Satinwood	109,000.
D	8' 11-3/4"	Santos Rosewood	116,300.
D	8' 11-3/4"	Pearwood	116,700.
D	8' 11-3/4"	East Indian Rosewood	117,300.
D	8' 11-3/4"	African Pommele	117,600.
D	8' 11-3/4"	Macassar Ebony	128,400.
D	8' 11-3/4"	Hepplewhite Dark Cherry	106,400.

*For explanation of terms and prices, please see pages 28–33.

Steinway & Sons (continued)

Grands (Hamburg)

I frequently get requests for prices of pianos made in Steinway's branch factory in Hamburg, Germany. Officially, these pianos are not sold in North America, but it is possible to order one through an American Steinway dealer, or to go to Europe and purchase one there. The following list shows approximately how much it would cost to purchase a Hamburg Steinway in Germany and have it shipped to the United States. The list was derived by taking the published retail price in Germany, subtracting the value-added tax not applicable to foreign purchasers, converting to U.S. dollars (the rate used here is 1 Euro = $0.90 [$1.00 = 1.11 Euros], but is obviously subject to change), and adding approximate charges for duty, air freight, crating, insurance, brokerage fees, and delivery. Only prices for grands in polished ebony are shown here. *Caution:* This list is published for general informational purposes only. The price that Steinway would charge for a piano ordered through an American Steinway dealer may be different. (Also, the cost of a trip to Germany to purchase the piano is not included!)

Model	Size	Style and Finish	Price
S-155	5' 1"	Polished Ebony	37,000.
M-170	5' 7"	Polished Ebony	40,600.
O-180	5' 10-1/2"	Polished Ebony	43,100.
A-188	6' 2"	Polished Ebony	46,100.
B-211	6' 11"	Polished Ebony	53,700.
C-227	7' 5-1/2"	Polished Ebony	62,900.
D-274	8' 11-3/4"	Polished Ebony *(estimated)*	80,400.

Story & Clark

Verticals

Model	Size	Style and Finish	Price
26062	44"	Continental Polished Ebony	2,790.
26070	44"	Continental Polished Mahogany	2,790.
27062	46"	Ebony	3,790.
28062	46"	Polished Ebony	3,390.
28070	46"	Polished Mahogany	3,390.
27060	46"	Walnut	3,790.
27050	46"	Oak	3,790.
26150/26250	46"	"Decorator" Oak	4,390.
26158/26258	46"	"Decorator" Cherry	4,390.

Model	Size	Style and Finish	Price*
26160/26260	46"	"Decorator" Walnut	4,390.
21262	47"	Ebony	3,990.
21270	47"	Mahogany	3,990.
21470	53"	Mahogany	5,990.

Grands

Model	Size	Style and Finish	Price*
20662	5'	Polished Ebony	7,590.
20670	5'	Polished Mahogany	8,190.
20666	5'	Polished Walnut	8,190.
20668	5'	Polished White	8,190.
20562	5' 4"	Polished Ebony	9,590.
20560	5' 4"	Polished Walnut	10,190.
20570	5' 4"	Polished Mahogany	10,190.
20762	6'	Polished Ebony	11,590.
20760	6'	Polished Walnut	12,190.
20770	6'	Polished Mahogany	12,190.

Strauss

Verticals

Model	Size	Style and Finish	Price*
UP-106	42"	Satin	3,590.
UP-108E	42-1/2"	Polished Ebony	3,190.
UP-108E	42-1/2"	Polished Mahogany	3,390.
UP-108E	42-1/2"	Polished Walnut	3,390.
UP-110A	43-1/2"	Polished Ebony	3,390.
UP-110A	43-1/2"	Polished Mahogany	3,590.
UP-110A	43-1/2"	Polished Walnut	3,590.
UP-110GD	43-1/2"	Satin	3,790.
UP-110GE	43-1/2"	Satin	3,790.
UP-117D,C	46"	Polished Ebony	3,590.
UP-117D,C	46"	Polished Mahogany	3,790.
UP-117D,C	46"	Polished Walnut	3,790.
UP-118	46-1/2"	Polished Ebony	3,790.
UP-118	46-1/2"	Polished Mahogany	3,990.
UP-118	46-1/2"	Polished Walnut	3,990.
UP-120E	47"	Satin	4,990.
UP-120E2,3	47"	Polished Maple	5,190.
UP-120H	47"	Polished Ebony	4,990.

*For explanation of terms and prices, please see pages 28–33.

Model	Size	Style and Finish	Price*

Strauss (continued)

Model	Size	Style and Finish	Price*
UP-122B	48"	Polished Ebony	3,990.
UP-122B	48"	Polished Mahogany	4,190.
UP-122B	48"	Polished Walnut	4,190.
UP-123	48"	Polished Ebony	5,390.
UP-125	49"	Polished Ebony	5,790.
Grands			
GP-170	5' 7"	Polished Ebony	11,990.

Walter, Charles R.

Verticals			
1520	43"	Oak	7,560.
1520	43"	Cherry	7,800.
1520	43"	Walnut	7,820.
1520	43"	Mahogany	7,960.
1520	43"	Riviera Oak	7,540.
1520	43"	Italian Provincial Oak	7,540.
1520	43"	Italian Provincial Walnut	7,840.
1520	43"	French Provincial Oak	7,840.
1520	43"	French Provincial Walnut	8,080.
1520	43"	French Provincial Cherry	8,100.
1520	43"	Country Classic Oak	7,600.
1520	43"	Country Classic Cherry	7,740.
1520	43"	Queen Anne Oak	7,900.
1520	43"	Queen Anne Cherry	8,100.
1520	43"	Queen Anne Mahogany	8,100.
1500	45"	Ebony	7,320.
1500	45"	Polished Ebony	7,700.
1500	45"	Oak	7,000.
1500	45"	Walnut	7,260.
1500	45"	Mahogany	7,480.
1500	45"	Cherry	7,480.
1500	45"	Gothic Oak	7,440.
Grands			
W-190	6' 4"	Ebony	32,800.

Model	Size	Style and Finish	Price*
W-190	6' 4"	Semi-Polished and Polished Ebony	33,600.
W-190	6' 4"	Mahogany	34,200.
W-190	6' 4"	Semi-Polished and Polished Mahogany	35,000.
W-190	6' 4"	Walnut	34,200.
W-190	6' 4"	Open-Pore Walnut	34,400.
W-190	6' 4"	Semi-Polished and Polished Walnut	35,000.
W-190	6' 4"	Cherry	34,200.
W-190	6' 4"	Semi-Polished and Polished Cherry	35,000.
W-190	6' 4"	Oak	31,500.
W-190	6' 4"	Chippendale Mahogany	35,200.
W-190	6' 4"	Chip. Semi-Pol. and Pol. Mahogany	36,000.
W-190	6' 4"	Chippendale Cherry	35,200.
W-190	6' 4"	Chip. Semi-Pol. and Pol. Cherry	36,000.

Weber

Model numbers with two digits designate models from Korea, with three digits, from China.

Verticals

Model	Size	Style and Finish	Price*
W-109	43"	Continental Polished Ebony	3,380.
W-109	43"	Continental Polished Walnut	3,500.
W-109	43"	Continental Polished Mahogany	3,500.
W-109	43"	Continental Polished White	3,440.
W-109	43"	Continental Polished Ivory	3,440.
WF-108	43-1/2"	French Cherry	3,900.
WF-108	43-1/2"	Mahogany	3,900.
WF-108	43-1/2"	Italian Walnut	3,900.
WF-108	43-1/2"	Mediterranean Oak	3,900.
WF-108	43-1/2"	Queen Anne Cherry	3,900.
WF-110	43-1/2"	French Cherry	4,300.
WF-110	43-1/2"	Mahogany	4,100.
WF-110	43-1/2"	Queen Anne Oak	4,300.
WSF-44	43-1/2"	French Cherry	6,790.
WSF-44	43-1/2"	Mediterranean Oak	6,790.
WSF-44	43-1/2"	Queen Anne Oak	6,790.
WSF-44	43-1/2"	Mahogany	6,790.
WSE-48	47"	Polished Ebony	6,390.

*For explanation of terms and prices, please see pages 28–33.

Model	Size	Style and Finish	Price*
Weber (continued)			
WSE-48	47"	Polished Mahogany	6,590.
WSE-48	47"	Polished Brown Mahogany	6,590.
WSE-48	47"	Polished Walnut	6,590.
W-121	48"	Polished Ebony	4,460.
W-121	48"	Polished Mahogany	4,580.
W-121	48"	Polished Walnut	4,580.
WF-121	48"	Walnut	4,780.
W-131	52"	Polished Ebony	4,880.
Grands			
WG-150	4' 11-1/2"	Polished Ebony	9,500.
WG-150	4' 11-1/2"	Polished Mahogany	9,700.
WG-150	4' 11-1/2"	Polished White	9,500.
WG-50	4' 11-1/2"	Ebony and Polished Ebony	11,980.
WG-50	4' 11-1/2"	Polished Walnut	12,860.
WG-50	4' 11-1/2"	Polished Mahogany	12,860.
WG-50	4' 11-1/2"	Polished Brown Mahogany	12,860.
WG-50	4' 11-1/2"	Cherry	13,260.
WG-50	4' 11-1/2"	Polished White	12,380.
WG-50	4' 11-1/2"	Polished Ivory	12,380.
WG-50	4' 11-1/2"	Queen Anne Polished Ebony	13,920.
WG-50	4' 11-1/2"	Queen Anne Polished Mahogany	14,900.
WG-50	4' 11-1/2"	Queen Anne Polished Brown Mahogany	14,900.
WG-50	4' 11-1/2"	Queen Anne Cherry	15,300.
WG-50	4' 11-1/2"	Queen Anne Oak	15,020.
WG-50	4' 11-1/2"	Queen Anne Polished Ivory	14,220.
WG-51	5' 1"	Ebony and Polished Ebony	13,000.
WG-51	5' 1"	Polished Walnut	13,720.
WG-51	5' 1"	Polished Mahogany	13,720.
WG-51	5' 1"	Polished Brown Mahogany	13,720.
WG-51	5' 1"	Cherry	14,120.
WSG-51	5' 1"	Polished Ebony	13,790.
WSG-51	5' 1"	Polished Mahogany	14,190.
WSG-51	5' 1"	Polished Brown Mahogany	14,190.
WSG-51	5' 1"	Empire Brown Mahogany	17,590.
WSG-51	5' 1"	Polished White	13,990.

Model	Size	Style and Finish	Price*
WG-157	5' 2"	Polished Ebony	10,500.
WG-157	5' 2"	Polished Mahogany	10,900.
WG-57	5' 7"	Ebony and Polished Ebony	15,120.
WG-57	5' 7"	Walnut and Polished Walnut	15,760.
WG-57	5' 7"	Polished Mahogany	15,760.
WG-57	5' 7"	Polished Brown Mahogany	15,760.
WG-57	5' 7"	Cherry	16,160.
WSG-57	5' 7"	Polished Ebony	15,790.
WSG-57	5' 7"	Polished Mahogany	16,390.
WSG-57	5' 7"	Polished Brown Mahogany	16,390.
WSG-57	5' 7"	Empire Brown Mahogany	19,390.
WSG-57	5' 7"	Polished Walnut	16,390.
WSG-57	5' 7"	Queen Anne Mahogany	18,790.
WSG-57	5' 7"	Queen Anne Cherry	18,990.
WG-175	5' 9"	Polished Ebony	11,300.
WG-60	6' 1"	Ebony and Polished Ebony	16,320.
WG-60	6' 1"	Polished Mahogany	16,660.
WG-60	6' 1"	Polished Walnut	16,660.
WSG-60	6' 1"	Polished Ebony	17,990.
WG-68	6' 10"	Ebony and Polished Ebony	21,200.
WG-70	7'	Ebony and Polished Ebony	26,300.
WG-90	9'	Ebony and Polished Ebony	62,090.

Weinbach

Note: Prices below do not include bench. Add from $220 to $630 (most are under $400), depending on choice of bench.

Verticals

114-I	45"	Demi-Chippendale Polished Walnut	6,180.
114-I	45"	Demi-Chippendale Pol.Flame Mahog.	6,180.
114-IC	45"	Chippendale Polished Walnut	6,500.
114-IC	45"	Chippendale Polished Flame Mahogany	6,500.
114-II	45"	Polished Ebony	5,500.
114-II	45"	Polished Walnut	5,500.
114-II	45"	Polished Flame Mahogany	5,500.
114-IV	45"	Polished Ebony	5,900.
114-IV	45"	Polished Walnut	5,900.
114-IV	45"	Polished Flame Mahogany	5,900.

*For explanation of terms and prices, please see pages 28–33.

Model	Size	Style and Finish	Price*

Weinbach (continued)

124-III	50"	Polished Ebony	7,100.
124-III	50"	Polished Walnut	7,100.
124-III	50"	Polished Flame Mahogany	7,100.
Grands			
155	5' 3"	Polished Ebony	18,780.
155	5' 3"	Polished Walnut	18,780.
155	5' 3"	Polished Flame Mahogany	18,780.
170	5' 8"	Polished Ebony	19,800.
170	5' 8"	Polished Walnut	19,800.
170	5' 8"	Polished Flame Mahogany	19,800.
170 C	5' 8"	Chippendale Polished Walnut	23,800.
170 C	5' 8"	Chippendale Polished Mahogany	23,800.
192	6' 4"	Polished Ebony	23,000.
192	6' 4"	Polished Walnut	23,000.
192	6' 4"	Polished Flame Mahogany	23,000.

Welmar

Prices are FOB England and do not include duty, freight, and other costs of importing. Oak, ash, and cherry are available at the same price as mahogany. Polished white is available at the same price as polished ebony.

Verticals

112	44"	Polished Ebony	10,770.
112	44"	Mahogany	9,270.
112	44"	Polished Mahogany	10,770.
112	44"	Walnut	9,270.
112	44"	Polished Walnut	10,770.
112	44"	Teak	9,270.
112 School	44"	Mahogany	9,840.
112 School	44"	Oak	9,840.
114	44"	Polished Ebony	11,010.
114	44"	Mahogany	9,675.
114	44"	Polished Mahogany	11,010.
114	44"	Walnut	9,675.
114	44"	Polished Walnut	11,010.

Model	Size	Style and Finish	Price*
114	44"	Teak	9,675.
114 Regency	44"	Mahogany	10,320.
114 Regency	44"	Polished Mahogany	11,610.
126	50"	Polished Ebony	12,795.
126	50"	Mahogany	11,625.
126	50"	Polished Mahogany	12,795.
126	50"	Walnut	11,625.
126	50"	Polished Walnut	12,795.
Grands			
186	6' 1"	Polished Ebony	37,785.

Westbrook / Brentwood

Verticals

CFR006	43"	Country French Walnut	2,790.
CFR006	43"	Country French Oak	2,790.
CFR006	43"	Country French Cherry	2,830.
TR006	43"	Walnut	2,790.
TR006	43"	Oak	2,790.
TR006	43"	Cherry	2,830.
MP005	43"	Polished Ebony	2,590.
MP005	43"	Polished Walnut	2,590.
MP005	43"	Polished Mahogany	2,590.
MP005	43"	Polished Cherry	2,590.
MP005	43"	Polished White	2,790.
MP012	48"	Polished Ebony	2,990.
MP012	48"	Polished Walnut	2,990.
MP012	48"	Polished Mahogany	2,990.
MP012	48"	Polished Cherry	2,990.

Wieler — see "Sängler & Söhne / Wieler"

*For explanation of terms and prices, please see pages 28–33.

Woodchester

Prices are FOB England and do not include duty, freight, and other costs of importing. Oak, ash, and cherry are available at the same price as mahogany. Polished white is available at the same price as polished ebony.

Verticals

Model	Size	Style and Finish	Price
Elmore	42"	Polished Ebony	5,640.
Elmore	42"	Mahogany	4,785.
Elmore	42"	Polished Mahogany	5,640.
Elmore	42"	Walnut	4,785.
Elmore	42"	Polished Walnut	5,640.
Elmore	42"	Teak	4,785.
Arlingham	46"	Polished Ebony	6,075.
Arlingham	46"	Mahogany	5,250.
Arlingham	46"	Polished Mahogany	6,075.
Arlingham	46"	Walnut	5,250.
Arlingham	46"	Polished Walnut	6,075.
Arlingham	46"	Teak	5,250.
Burleigh	46"	Polished Ebony	9,375.
Burleigh	46"	Mahogany	8,220.
Burleigh	46"	Polished Mahogany	9,375.
Burleigh	46"	Walnut	8,220.
Burleigh	46"	Polished Walnut	9,375.
Burleigh	46"	Teak	8,220.
Kingscourt	46"	Polished Ebony	6,300.
Kingscourt	46"	Mahogany	5,385.
Kingscourt	46"	Polished Mahogany	6,300.
Kingscourt	46"	Walnut	5,385.
Kingscourt	46"	Polished Walnut	6,300.
Kingscourt	46"	Teak	5,385.
Concerto	48"	Polished Ebony	10,620.
Concerto	48"	Mahogany	9,435.
Concerto	48"	Polished Mahogany	10,620.
Concerto	48"	Walnut	9,435.
Concerto	48"	Polished Walnut	10,620.
Concerto	48"	Teak	9,435.
Gloucester	50"	Polished Ebony	7,890.
Gloucester	50"	Mahogany	6,765.

Model	Size	Style and Finish	Price*
Gloucester	50"	Polished Mahogany	7,890.
Gloucester	50"	Walnut	6,765.
Gloucester	50"	Polished Walnut	7,890.
Gloucester	50"	Teak	6,765.

Wurlitzer

Verticals

Model	Size	Style and Finish	Price
1175A	37"	American Country Regal Oak	3,660.
1176N	37"	Queen Anne Royal Cherry	3,660.
2270A	42"	Vintage Mahogany	3,940.
2275B	42"	American Country Regal Oak	3,940.
2276B	42"	Queen Anne Royal Cherry	3,940.
WP50	42"	Continental Polished Ebony	2,790.
WP50	42"	Continental Polished Cherry	2,790.
WP60	47"	Polished Ebony	3,390.
WP60	47"	Polished Mahogany	3,390.

Grands

Model	Size	Style and Finish	Price
C143	4' 7"	Ebony and Polished Ebony	9,028.
C143	4' 7"	Polished Mahogany	9,298.
C143	4' 7"	Polished Oak	9,298.
C143	4' 7"	Polished White	9,028.
C153	5' 1"	Ebony and Polished Ebony	10,440.
C153	5' 1"	Polished Mahogany	10,800.
C153	5' 1"	Walnut	10,800.
C153	5' 1"	Oak	10,800.
C153	5' 1"	Polished Ivory	10,440.
C153QA	5' 1"	Queen Anne Polished Mahogany	12,600.
C153QA	5' 1"	Queen Anne Oak	12,600.
C153QA	5' 1"	Queen Anne Cherry	12,600.
C173	5' 8"	Ebony and Polished Ebony	11,520.
C173	5' 8"	Polished Mahogany	11,872.
C173	5' 8"	Polished White	11,520.

*For explanation of terms and prices, please see pages 28–33.

Model	Size	Style and Finish	Price*
Yamaha			
Verticals			
M112	44"	Continental Ebony	5,090.
M112	44"	Continental Polished Ebony	5,190.
M112	44"	Continental American Walnut	5,290.
M112	44"	Continental Polished Mahogany	6,390.
M112	44"	Continental Polished White	6,290.
M450	44"	American Oak	3,790.
M450	44"	Cherry	3,790.
M500	44"	Cottage Cherry	4,890.
M500	44"	Country Manor Light Oak	6,390.
M500	44"	Country Villa White Oak	6,590.
M500	44"	Florentine Light Oak	4,890.
M500	44"	Georgian Mahogany	5,990.
M500	44"	Hancock Brown Cherry	4,290.
M500	44"	Milano Dark Oak	4,890.
M500	44"	Parisian Cherry	6,190.
M500	44"	Queen Anne Cherry	5,090.
M500	44"	Queen Anne Dark Cherry	5,090.
M500	44"	Sheraton Mahogany	4,290.
P22	45"	American Walnut	5,190.
P22	45"	Black Oak	5,190.
P22	45"	Dark Oak	5,190.
P22	45"	Light Oak	5,190.
T116	45"	Polished Ebony	5,390.
T116	45"	Polished Mahogany	6,390.
T121	48"	Polished Ebony	6,390.
U1	48"	Ebony	7,790.
U1	48"	Polished Ebony	7,990.
U1	48"	American Walnut	8,390.
U1	48"	Polished American Walnut	8,990.
U1	48"	Polished Mahogany	8,990.
U1	48"	Polished White	9,190.
U3	52"	Polished Ebony	10,690.
U3	52"	Polished Mahogany	11,990.
U5	52"	Polished Ebony	12,590.

Model	Size	Style and Finish	Price*
U5	52"	Bubinga	21,990.
U5C	52"	*"Centennial" Pol. Mahog. w/Flower Inlays*	25,990.
Disklavier Verticals			
MX500	44"	Country Manor Light Oak	11,190.
MX500	44"	Country Villa White Oak	11,390.
MX500	44"	Florentine Light Oak	9,790
MX500	44"	Georgian Mahogany	10,790.
MX500	44"	Milano Dark Oak	9,790
MX500	44"	Parisian Cherry	10,990.
MX500	44"	Parisian Dark Cherry	10,990
MX500	44"	Queen Anne Cherry	9,990.
MX500	44"	Queen Anne Dark Cherry	9,990.
MX22	45"	American Walnut	10,190.
MX22	45"	Dark Oak	10,190.
MX22	45"	Black Oak	10,190.
MX22	45"	Light Oak	10,190.
MX116	45"	Polished Ebony	10,390.
MX116	45"	Polished Mahogany	11,390
MIDIPiano (Silent) Verticals			
MP500	44"	Cottage Cherry	7,590.
MP500	44"	Country Manor Light Oak	8,990.
MP500	44"	Country Villa White Oak	9,190.
MP500	44"	Florentine Light Oak	7,590.
MP500	44"	Georgian Mahogany	8,590.
MP500	44"	Hancock Brown Cherry	7,090.
MP500	44"	Milano Dark Oak	7,590.
MP500	44"	Parisian Cherry	8,790.
MP500	44"	Queen Anne Cherry	7,790.
MP500	44"	Queen Anne Dark Cherry	7,790.
MP500	44"	Sheraton Mahogany	7,090.
MP22	45"	American Walnut	7,790.
MP1Z	48"	Polished Ebony	10,590.
Disklavier Verticals with Silent Feature			
MPX1Z	48"	Polished Ebony	15,290.
MPX1Z	48"	American Walnut	15,690.
MPX1Z	48"	*Polished Mahogany*	16,290.
MPX1Z	48"	Polished White	16,490.

*For explanation of terms and prices, please see pages 28–33.

Model	Size	Style and Finish	Price*

Yamaha (continued)

Grands

Model	Size	Style and Finish	Price*
GA1E	4' 11"	Polished Ebony	9,990.
GC1	5' 3"	Ebony	14,490.
GC1	5' 3"	Polished Ebony	14,890.
GC1	5' 3"	American Walnut	16,490.
GC1	5' 3"	Polished American Walnut	16,490.
GC1	5' 3"	Polished Mahogany	16,490.
GC1	5' 3"	Polished Ivory	16,490.
GC1	5' 3"	Polished White	16,090.
GH1FP	5' 3"	French Provincial Cherry	20,090.
GH1G	5' 3"	Georgian Mahogany	20,090.
C1	5' 3"	Ebony	18,690.
C1	5' 3"	Polished Ebony	19,090.
C1	5' 3"	American Walnut	21,390.
C1	5' 3"	Mahogany and Polished Mahogany	22,190.
C1	5' 3"	Polished White	21,390.
C1	5' 3"	"Metro" Polished Ebony and Gold	21,590.
C2	5' 8"	Ebony	21,390.
C2	5' 8"	Polished Ebony	21,590.
C2	5' 8"	American Walnut	24,390.
C2	5' 8"	Polished American Walnut	25,190.
C2	5' 8"	Polished Mahogany	25,190.
C2	5' 8"	Light American Oak	24,390.
C2	5' 8"	Polished White	23,090.
C3	6' 1"	Ebony	29,090.
C3	6' 1"	Polished Ebony	29,290.
C3	6' 1"	American Walnut	32,090.
C3	6' 1"	Polished Mahogany	32,690.
C3	6' 1"	NEO Aluminum and Cherry	83,990.
C3	6' 1"	Bubinga	55,990.
C3	6' 1"	Bubinga Floral	57,990.
C3C	6' 1"	*"Centennial" Pol. Mahog. w/Flower Inlays*	77,210.
S4	6' 3"	Polished Ebony	52,490.
C5	6' 7"	Ebony	31,390.
C5	6' 7"	Polished Ebony	31,590.
C6	6' 11"	Ebony	34,790.
C6	6' 11"	Polished Ebony	34,990.
S6	6' 11"	Polished Ebony	59,390.

Model	Size	Style and Finish	Price*
C7	7' 6"	Ebony	39,690.
C7	7' 6"	Polished Ebony	40,090.
CFIIIS	9'	Polished Ebony	108,390.

Disklavier Grands

Model	Size	Style and Finish	Price*
DGA1	4' 11"	Polished Ebony (playback only)	19,990.
DGC1A	5' 3"	*Ebony*	28,130.
DGC1A	5' 3"	Polished Ebony	28,530.
DGC1A	5' 3"	American Walnut	30,130.
DGC1A	5' 3"	*Polished American Walnut*	30,130.
DGC1A	5' 3"	*Polished Mahogany*	30,130.
DGC1A	5' 3"	*Polished Ivory*	30,130.
DGC1A	5' 3"	Polished White	29,730.
DC1A	5' 3"	*Ebony*	32,330.
DC1A	5' 3"	Polished Ebony	32,730.
DC1A	5' 3"	American Walnut	35,030.
DC1A	5' 3"	*Polished American Walnut*	35,830.
DC1A	5' 3"	*Polished Mahogany*	35,830.
DC1A	5' 3"	*Polished Ivory*	35,830.
DC1A	5' 3"	*Polished White*	35,030.
DC1A	5' 3"	"Metro" Polished Ebony and Gold	35,230.
DC2A	5' 8"	*Ebony*	35,030.
DC2A	5' 8"	Polished Ebony	35,230.
DC2A	5' 8"	American Walnut	38,030.
DC2A	5' 8"	*Polished American Walnut*	38,830.
DC2A	5' 8"	*Polished Mahogany*	38,830.
DC2A	5' 8"	Polished White	36,730.
DC3A	6' 1"	*Ebony*	43,330.
DC3A	6' 1"	Polished Ebony	43,530.
DC3A	6' 1"	American Walnut	46,330.
DC3A	6' 1"	*Polished Mahogany*	46,930.
DC3A	6' 1"	NEO Aluminum and Cherry	98,230.
DC3A	6' 1"	Bubinga	70,230.
DC3A	6' 1"	Bubinga Floral	72,230.
DC3A	6' 1"	Polished White	45,530.
DC5A	6' 7"	Ebony	45,630.
DC5A	6' 7"	Polished Ebony	45,830.
DC6A	6' 11"	Ebony	49,030.
DC6A	6' 11"	Polished Ebony	49,230.
DC7A	7' 6"	Ebony	53,930.
DC7A	7' 6"	Polished Ebony	54,330.

*For explanation of terms and prices, please see pages 28–33.

Yamaha (continued)

Disklavier Pro Grands

DC3APRO	6' 1"	Polished Ebony	51,490.
DS4APRO	6' 3"	Polished Ebony	76,890.
DC5APRO	6' 7"	Polished Ebony	53,790.
DC6APRO	6' 11"	Polished Ebony	57,190.
DS6APRO	6' 11"	Polished Ebony	83,790.
DC7APRO	7' 6"	Polished Ebony	64,090.
DCFIIISAPRO	9'	Polished Ebony	137,700.

MIDIPiano (Silent) Grands

MPC1	5' 3"	Polished Ebony	24,290.
MPC2	5' 8"	Polished Ebony	26,790.
MPC3	6' 1"	Polished Ebony	34,390.
MPC6	6' 11"	Polished Ebony	40,190.
MPC7	7' 6"	Polished Ebony	45,190.

Young Chang

See also under "Bergmann" and "Pramberger."

Verticals

PE-102	43"	Continental Polished Ebony	3,560.
PE-102	43"	Continental Polished Red Mahogany	3,980.
PE-102	43"	Continental Polished Brown Mahogany	3,980.
PF-110	43-1/2"	Mahogany	4,940.
PF-110	43-1/2"	Queen Anne Oak	5,150.
PF-110	43-1/2"	Mediterranean Oak	5,360.
PF-110	43-1/2"	Queen Anne Cherry	5,570.
PF-110	43-1/2"	French Provincial Cherry	5,780.
PF-110	43-1/2"	Apple Brown Satin	5,780.
PF-116	46-1/2"	Mediterranean Oak	6,080.
PF-116	46-1/2"	French Provincial Cherry	6,290.
PE-116S	46-1/2"	Ebony	5,030.
PE-116S	46-1/2"	American Walnut	5,240.
PE-116S	46-1/2"	American Oak	5,240.
PE-116S	46-1/2"	American Cherry	5,240.
PE-118	47"	Ebony and Polished Ebony	4,940.
PE-118	47"	Polished Red Mahogany	5,240.
PE-118	47"	Polished Brown Mahogany	5,240.
PE-121	48"	Ebony and Polished Ebony	5,150.

Model	Size	Style and Finish	Price*
PE-121	48"	Polished Red Mahogany	5,450.
PE-121	48"	Brown Mahog. and Pol. Brown Mahog.	5,450.
PE-131	52"	Polished Ebony	6,290.
Grands			
PG-150	4' 11-1/2"	Ebony and Polished Ebony	12,590.
PG-150	4' 11-1/2"	Polished Red Mahogany	13,220.
PG-150	4' 11-1/2"	Polished Brown Mahogany	13,220.
PG-150	4' 11-1/2"	Cherry	13,430.
PG-150	4' 11-1/2"	Polished Ivory	13,010.
PG-150	4' 11-1/2"	Polished White	13,010.
PG-150D	4' 11-1/2"	Queen Anne Polished Mahogany	15,530.
PG-150D	4' 11-1/2"	Queen Anne Cherry	15,740.
PG-150D	4' 11-1/2"	Queen Anne Polished Ivory	15,320.
PG-150KPS	4' 11-1/2"	Polished Ebony Kurzweil Player System	22,040.
PG-157	5' 2"	Ebony and Polished Ebony	14,180.
PG-157	5' 2"	Polished Red Mahogany	14,600.
PG-157	5' 2"	Polished Brown Mahogany	14,600.
PG-157	5' 2"	Cherry	14,810.
PG-157	5' 2"	Polished Ivory	14,390.
PG-157	5' 2"	Polished White	14,390.
PG-157D	5' 2"	Country French Cherry	17,630.
PG-157D	5' 2"	Queen Anne Mahogany	17,420.
PG-157D	5' 2"	Queen Anne Cherry	17,630.
PG-157D	5' 2"	Empire Polished Brown Mahogany	18,260.
PG-175	5' 9"	Ebony and Polished Ebony	16,160.
PG-175	5' 9"	Polished Red Mahogany	16,790.
PG-175	5' 9"	Polished Brown Mahogany	16,790.
PG-175	5' 9"	Walnut	16,790.
PG-175	5' 9"	American Cherry	16,790.
PG-175D	5' 9"	Empire Polished Brown Mahogany	20,360.
PG-185	6' 1"	Ebony and Polished Ebony	18,470.
PG-185	6' 1"	Walnut and Polished Walnut	19,430.
PG-185	6' 1"	Polished Red Mahogany	19,430.
PG-185	6' 1"	Polished Brown Mahogany	19,430.
PG-185	6' 1"	Polished Ivory	19,220.
PG-208	6' 10"	Ebony and Polished Ebony	23,090.
PG-213	7'	Ebony and Polished Ebony	28,550.
G-275	9'	Polished Ebony	65,300.

*For explanation of terms and prices, please see pages 28–33.

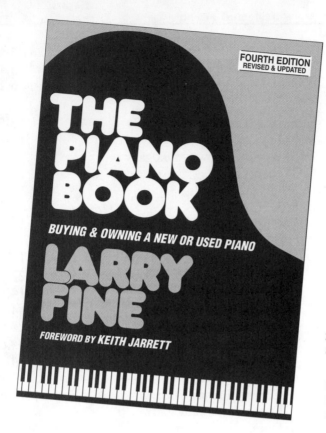

244 pages
8-1/2 x 11
100 line drawings

Hardcover $27.95
Paperback $19.95
Shipping/handling $5.00

- *Candid brand-by-brand reviews of new pianos*

- *Sales gimmicks to watch out for—and the real differences in piano quality and features*

- *How to negotiate the best deal*

- *Tips on finding, inspecting, appraising, and buying a used piano*

- *Special section on buying an older Steinway*

- *Piano moving, storage, tuning, servicing*